Creative
TERRARIUMS

Creative TERRARIUMS

33 MODERN MINI-GARDENS FOR YOUR HOME

Enid G. Svymbersky

FOX CHAPEL
PUBLISHING

Project Team
Vice President–Content: Christopher Reggio
Acquisition Editor: Bud Sperry
Editor: Jeremy Hauck
Copy Editor: Amy Deputato
Design: Llara Pazdan
Index: Jay Kreider

ISBN 978-1-56523-984-5

Library of Congress Cataloging-in-Publication Data

Names: Svymbersky, Enid G., author.
Title: Creative terrariums / Enid G. Svymbersky.
Description: Mount Joy, PA : Fox Chapel Publishing, 2019. | Includes index.
Identifiers: LCCN 2018051102| ISBN 9781565239845 (pbk.) | ISBN 9781607656401
  (ebook)
Subjects: LCSH: Terrariums. | Glass gardens. | Indoor gardening.
Classification: LCC SB417 .S89 2019 | DDC 635.9/824--dc23
LC record available at https://lccn.loc.gov/2018051102

To learn more about the other great books from Fox Chapel Publishing,
or to find a retailer near you, call toll-free
800-457-9112 or visit us at *www.FoxChapelPublishing.com*.

We are always looking for talented authors. To submit an idea,
please send a brief inquiry to acquisitions@foxchapelpublishing.com.

Printed in Singapore
First printing

CONTENTS

INTRODUCTION

I grew up in a not-so-bad, but also not-so-nice, part of Los Angeles. Describing it as "concrete jungle" would be putting it mildly. Trees, hedges, and flowerbeds were practically nonexistent in my neighborhood. That is, until you reached my house. Picture a perfectly manicured lawn, multicolored rose bushes and hydrangeas, and an incorrigible rubber tree that needed pruning all the time, not to mention a ginormous avocado tree in the backyard that could be seen from the street threatening to devour the power lines. The neighbors hated us. They lived in constant fear that our trees' roots would crack their precious concrete. They were a constant nuisance to my parents. On the flip side, we frequently had strangers knocking on our door asking for avocados and growing advice. These were more our type of people and I always watched my grandparents or parents (depending on who was home) invite them inside. The inside of our house was no different from the outside. My grandmother's devil's ivy *(Epipremnum aureum)* grew rampant all over the living room. In true jungle fashion, it trailed up the walls and around the perimeter of the ceiling in the most breathtaking way. Anyone we invited into our home was instantly fascinated by our wacky way of life.

Always chasing greener pastures, I attended UC Davis, a school known for agriculture and its arboretum that spans more than 5,300 acres. To this day, I have never lived on a greener patch of heaven on earth than during those years. If I was better at math I would probably be telling you about my days learning about chemistry and botany, but instead I was most at home at the school's craft center. In exchange for free classes, I volunteered to check out tools to the woodworkers, sell clay to the wheel throwers, and set up the chemical baths for the photographers. This is when crafting and making things with my hands really became a passion for me.

Years later, I decided to do what everybody does when they have a passion for something: I started a blog! Living in Los Angeles again, and working a 9-to-5 job, I needed a

creative outlet. I was fortunate to find an online community of crafters and plant enthusiasts who felt the same way I did. Then opportunity struck—not for me, but for my husband. He was offered a great job in the San Francisco Bay Area, so we immediately packed our bags and moved . . . into a 130-square-foot room while we figured out where to live. I very quickly realized that I had never been so devoid of greenery in my life. How could we survive six months in a boring, confined room

I would love to share your finished terrarium designs! #creativeterrariumsbook

like this? To bring a little life to the place I started creating mini aeriums (air plant terrariums) and succulent terrariums. No clear container was safe from me! I used whatever I could get my hands on: glass jars, bowls, plastic bottles . . . I even transformed our mini coffeepot into an air plant terrarium (see page 28). I thought it was the sweetest little thing, and I couldn't just keep it to myself. I decided to post the picture on my blog, and, before I knew it, it was all over social media. That moment of creativity born of my desperation for some greenery in my life is how I came to write *Creative Terrariums*.

Maybe you picked up this book because you live in a small apartment and feel that a terrarium would be the perfect complement to your space, or maybe you love the challenge of a good DIY project with your kids, or maybe you've killed one too many houseplants (it's okay, we've all been there), and now you're ready to give terrariums a try!

In these pages you'll be introduced to 33 step-by-step terrarium projects featuring cacti, succulents, tropical plants, mosses, and air plants, to get you started. You will learn everything you need to know to choose the right vessel, foundation, plants, and decorative elements to confidently bring your own mini landscapes to life. You will learn how to identify symptoms of illness and methods for saying "buh-bye" to unwanted pests. We'll also cover general care tips and techniques to maintain your terrarium.

Whatever the reason behind you holding this book in your hands, please know that I'm beyond humbled, and I sincerely want to thank you for joining me on this adventure. I wish you lots of fun and happy plant memories ahead.

—ENID

You will learn how to identify symptoms of illness and methods for saying "buh-bye" to unwanted pests.

THE WARDIAN CASE
A HISTORY OF TERRARIUMS

I've heard of some fanatical obsessions sweeping a nation but none of them can light a candle to the 19th-century Victorian infatuation with ferns. In fact, the compulsion ran so deep it was given a name, *Pteridomania* (*pterido* being the Latin word for fern, and *mania*, well . . . you can guess). Ferns were so much a part of Victorian life that fern motifs were printed on every decorative façade imaginable: buildings, fences, furniture, pottery, tea sets, clothing, and even tombstones donned the fronds.

Nathaniel Bagshaw Ward
(1791–1868)

Fern fever even offered young women a little social independence. During this era, it became perfectly acceptable for women to explore the outdoors on fern-hunting expeditions, sans chaperone! As you can probably imagine, the boys were not too far behind. Over the years, these social occasions reportedly led to many a fern-induced love affair. So just how did this frenzy take over an entire nation?

Dr. Nathaniel Bagshaw Ward, a London physician and nature enthusiast, could not for the life of him keep his ferns alive. He yearned for an indoor garden but the increasing smog from industrialization and the infamous London fog proved to be less-than-ideal conditions—until one day, to his utter amazement, he found a young fern growing inside one of his sealed jars. Dr. Ward discovered that the fern thrived in a closed and humid environment. This observation piqued his interest, so to conduct further experiments he called on a carpenter to build him a small airtight greenhouse made of wood and glass. This "Wardian Case," as it would eventually come

Wardian Cases

> *"Know from whence you came. If you know whence you came, there are absolutely no limitations to where you can go."*
> —James Baldwin

to be called, is how the first terrarium of the modern era was born.

Dr. Ward shared his findings with his friends in the botany community, and before he knew it, fern fever was in full swing. Wardian Cases were manufactured in all sizes, from small portable cases for the amateur home collector to giant life-size versions called "ferneries." Most significantly, Wardian Cases were instrumental in transporting live specimens across long ocean voyages. Thousands of Wardian Cases were used to import live tea trees from China to England, and we all know how much the Brits love their tea! Rubber trees were fetched from Brazil, which led to a prosperous rubber industry that played a crucial role in both World Wars.

However, as the saying goes, all good things must come to an end, and by the beginning of the 20th century the popularity of ferns dwindled and was subsequently replaced by orchid fever. Dr. Ward was certainly not the first person to invent the science behind a terrarium, but he certainly championed the cause and made plant collecting more accessible to the masses. In the end, what I find so remarkable is that all of this was born from nothing more than a little fern in a jar.

According to the American Fern Society, today there are over 10,000 species of ferns.

Ferns are common enough that they are readily available for purchase at most garden centers and even farmers markets. In parts of the southern United States, Kimberly queen ferns adorn entranceways and Boston ferns hang from porch baskets. In New England, fiddlehead ferns are harvested in the spring and then cooked and served as a delectable regional specialty. With the popularity of terrariums on the rise, ferns are once again making their way under glass enclosures for our viewing pleasure!

A hanging Boston fern.

HOW A TERRARIUM WORKS

WHAT IS A TERRARIUM?

Terrariums are an eye-catching way to bring the whimsy of nature indoors. These mini indoor gardens are a great way to maximize space while adding a touch of greenery to your home. The conventional definition of a *terrarium* is a self-sustaining living ecosystem inside a sealed glass container. The high humidity inside an airtight container provides the right conditions for many tropical plants to thrive in your home all year long.

While there are some extraordinary exceptions, terrarium displays are not forever. Even with regular pruning and maintenance, plants tend to outgrow their containers and need to be repotted into larger containers. This means you get to go out and buy new plants for a new display, and that can be really exciting!

Take into consideration that not all plants can be kept under glass and not all species can be planted together in a terrarium. Tropical plants are best suited for closed containers while succulents, tillandsias, and cacti need the airflow that an open vessel provides. While not all the terrariums in this book are conventional terrariums (in fact most stray far off the beaten path), it's important to understand some fundamental workings of a biosphere to really appreciate how amazing it is to cultivate life under glass.

Everything happening inside a terrarium is a miniature representation of all the amazing phenomena we experience in our own natural world. I've found that having some knowledge of plant biology is very helpful in maintaining healthy plants indoors. While we all learn about photosynthesis and the water cycle in grade school, I thought a little refresher would be helpful.

Carbon Dioxide (CO_2) + Water (H_2O) + Sunlight = Sugar (Glucose) + Oxygen (O_2)

PHOTOSYNTHESIS

Plants create their own food through a process called *photosynthesis*. In the Greek language, *photo* means "light," and *synthesis* means "to combine." Plants combine water and carbon dioxide and use the energy from the sun to create their food. Plants have tiny openings in their leaves called *stomata* which open to collect carbon dioxide from the air. The water molecules from the roots and carbon dioxide from the leaves are then transported to the plant's chloroplast cells where sunlight is collected. Here food is created for the plant in the form of sugar (glucose). Oxygen is a byproduct of this process (it's lucky for us that it is) and at night the plant releases oxygen into the air through the process of respiration. Because it's not polite to disturb plants during respiration, if you must add water to your terrarium or water your houseplants in general, try to do it in the morning.

CRISPY BROWN LEAVES

Q: What does it mean when leaves, especially along the edges, turn brown and crispy?

A: From what we know about transpiration and evaporation, water from the leaves is evaporating faster than the plant can transport water from the roots to the leaves, leaving them to dry out and lose their vibrant color. Your plants could be suffering from the soil being too dry, the air being too dry, or getting too much sunlight. Prune crispy leaves to allow the plant to focus its energy on healthy foliage.

THE WATER CYCLE

The water cycle is what sustains all life here on Earth. Without the water cycle, we would not have clouds or rain to provide fresh water to all living things. This process can be summarized into three different stages: evaporation, condensation, and precipitation. As the sun heats up our oceans, lakes, and rivers, water vapor is created through the process of evaporation. This warm water vapor rises into our atmosphere where it meets cooler temperatures. During the condensation stage, water vapor cools and transforms into clouds. Clouds become saturated with liquid water molecules and, when they can hold no more water, they release it back down to earth as precipitation. Rain, hail, and snow collect in bodies of water, and the cycle begins again.

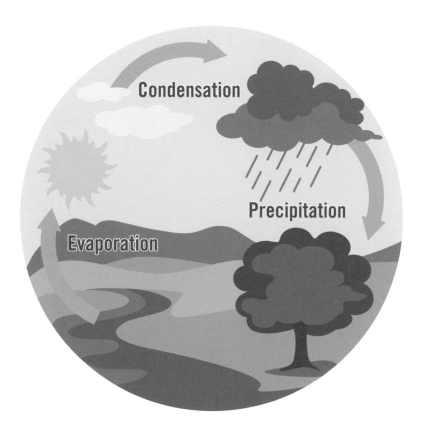

THE WATER CYCLE INSIDE A TERRARIUM

The water cycle inside a terrarium is not much different than the one outside. The three stages are transpiration, evaporation, and condensation. In a terrarium, the glass vessel takes the place of our atmosphere by holding the soil, water, and all living things inside. First, water is transported from the roots through the plant's leaves and released into the air through their leaves in a process called "transpiration." As the sun heats up the vessel, water is evaporated into the air. If you look closely you may even see a light mist or fog inside. As the air inside the terrarium becomes humid, or saturated with water vapor, it starts to condense and create liquid water on the glass. Eventually the water slides down and back into the soil. The water is recycled over and over so there is no need to continuously water a closed terrarium.

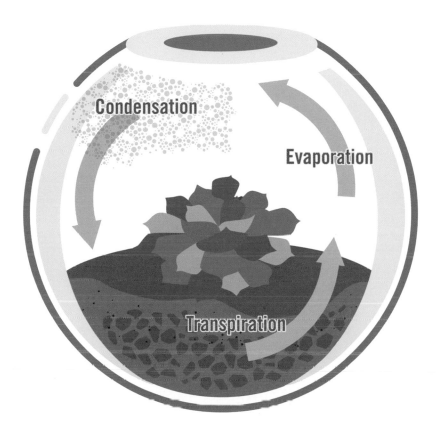

SHOW ME THE LAYERS

Terrarium vessels do not have drainage holes, so it's up to you to create a proper drainage system for your living display. In closed terrariums these layers play a crucial role in the water cycle. In an open container, they ensure proper drainage and keep plant roots from sitting in

1: DRAINAGE **2: SEPARATION** **3: FILTRATION** **4: SU**

PEBBLES SPHAGNUM MOSS HORTICULTURAL CHARCOAL SO

water for too long. The layers are presented in the order they should be followed. Of course, there is always a little room for creative interpretation.

RATE   **5: PLANTS**   **6: TOPDRESSING**   **7: DECORATIVE**

IX   **SUCCULENT**   **SAND**   **SHELLS**

LAYER ONE: DRAINAGE

This layer is also called a false bottom or water reservoir. It prevents plant roots from sitting in water, which can lead to rotting. Water percolates down into this layer until it can evaporate.

Drainage Mediums

- pebbles
- sand
- gravel

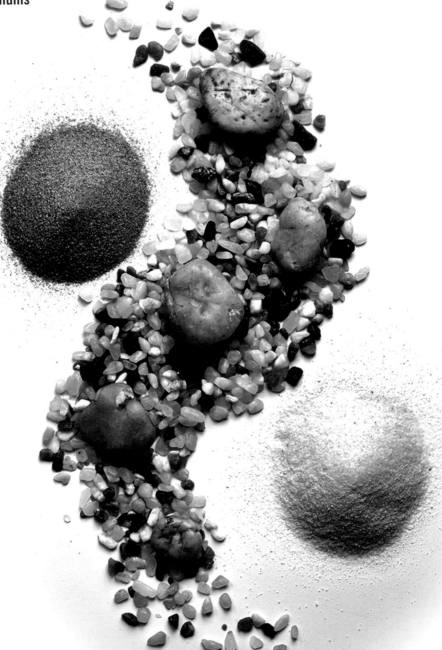

LAYER TWO: SEPARATION

This layer is optional but effective! It prevents the soil layer from falling into the drainage layer. This can get messy and take away from the overall appearance. Dried sphagnum moss is a popular choice for this layer. Before placing dried sphagnum moss into any terrarium project, first soak the moss in water for 10 minutes and then squeeze and drain out the excess water and let the moss dry. My favorite medium to use for this layer is fiberglass mesh. Hardware stores sell this mesh in rolls and the tiny holes in the screen allow water to easily pass through but deter the soil from falling through to the bottom. (Turn to the next page to see how to prepare it.)

Separation Mediums

- dried sphagnum moss
- butcher paper
- fiberglass screen sheet (window or fly screen)

HOW TO CUT FIBERGLASS MESH

Place your container on the screen. Use a marker to trace around the container and cut the screen.

If you don't want the screen to show as prominently through the glass, you can cut it slightly smaller than the size of the container.

LAYER THREE: FILTRATION

This layer is used to filter the water that will come down through the substrate layer. Horticultural charcoal will help keep mold from growing inside the terrarium. It will also keep the terrarium smelling fresh and do away with that mildew-like scent that can sometimes accompany damp areas.

Filtration Medium

- horticultural charcoal

LAYER FOUR: SUBSTRATE

This layer is for the soil. The type of soil medium depends on the type of plants used. Some tropical plants prefer more acidic soil than others. We'll talk more about the most suitable soil for your plants in the foundation section (see page 58). This substrate layer should be similar in depth to your drainage layer. Soil can become very saturated with water before it begins to percolate to the bottom. If the water reservoir is too shallow it will flood, and the roots of your plants will stay wet. This can lead to root rot and unfortunately kill your plants.

Substrate Mediums

- potting soil
- succulents and cacti soil mix
- pcat moss soil mix
- orchid soil mix

LAYER FIVE: PLANTS

After you have layered the foundation of the terrarium it's time to add your plants. The types of plants you use depend on the type of vessel. Remove plants from their pots, clean away any excess soil from the roots, and place them directly in the soil. Then cover the roots with soil, and pat down firmly.

Closed Terrarium Plants

- ferns
- mosses
- tropical plants

Open Terrarium Plants

- tillandsias (air plants)
- cacti
- succulents

LAYER SIX: TOPDRESSING

This layer is purely decorative. You can cover the substrate layer with a more attractive topper. Use a bamboo skewer or wood dowel to spread the medium between plants and cover the soil completely.

Topdressing Mediums

- sand
- pebbles
- crushed glass
- crushed seashells

LAYER SEVEN: DECORATIVE ELEMENTS

Decorative elements are not always necessary but they can add character to a themed terrarium!

Decorative Mediums

- seashells
- figurines
- crystals
- rocks
- sea fans
- reindeer moss

PART 1: GETTING STARTED

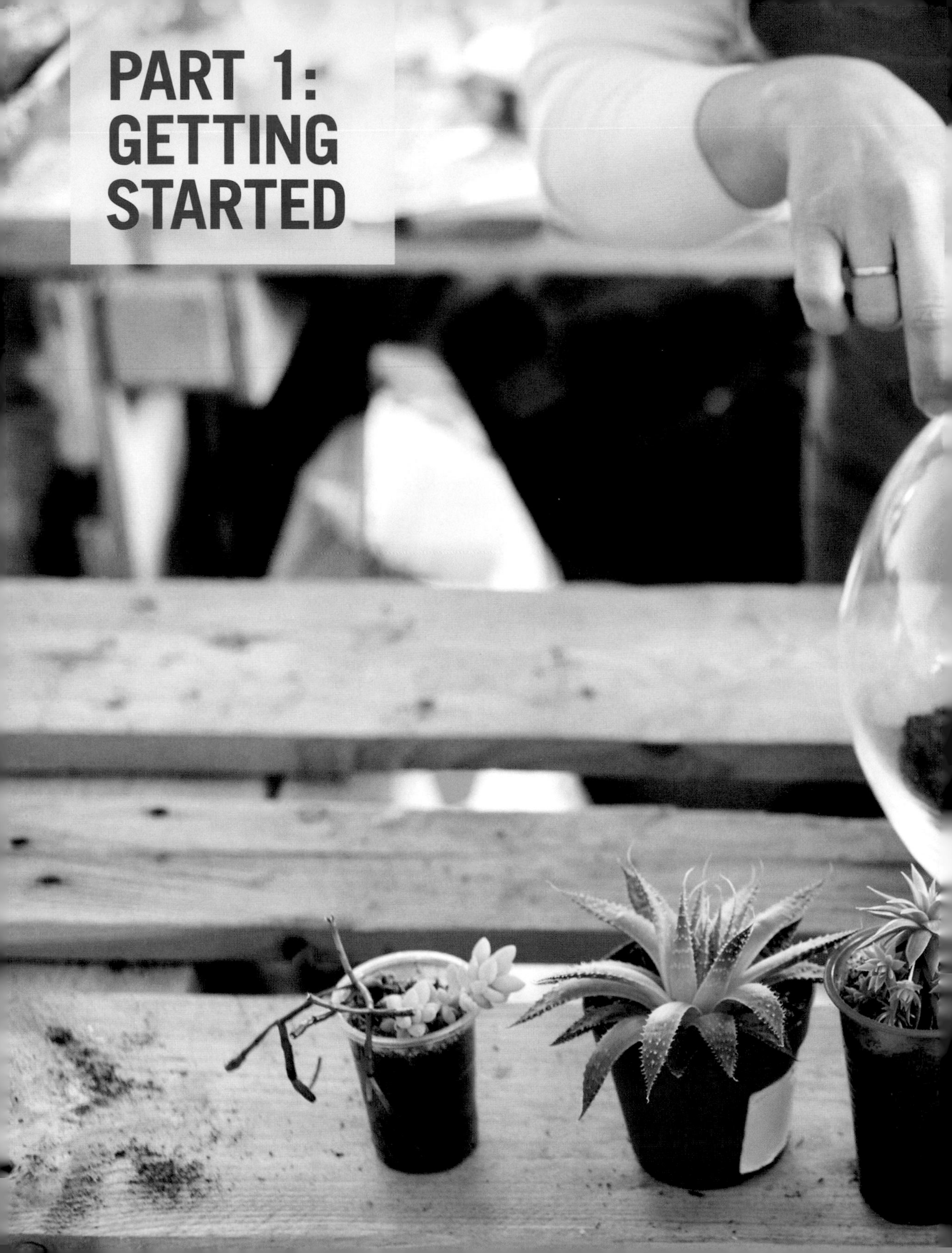

VESSELS

LOCATION, LOCATION, LOCATION

Traditionally, when we think of terrariums, we picture thick green foliage in a sealed glass vessel. But let's face it: there are so many more options for displaying plants these days that it's worth breaking the mold. Before deciding on an appropriate vessel for your terrarium, you'll want to ask yourself a few questions: Where will the terrarium live? On a nightstand, so it's the first thing you see in the morning? On a coffee table, for all to see? Are you all out of counter space? Then how about suspended from a wall or ceiling? Once you have the location all figured out, think about what type of vessel would work best in that space. A vessel with a flat bottom works best on a shelf, a vessel offering unobstructed 360-degree views is the perfect centerpiece for a coffee table, and a vessel with a hook is perfect for stringing up anywhere around your home.

On average, mosses prefer some shade, so be sure to relocate any moss terrariums from window ledges after you're finished admiring them. Succulents, on the other hand, love lots of sun.

The coffeepot terrarium that started it all for me!

REPURPOSED VESSELS

I'm constantly on the hunt for a drainage-free, watertight, transparent beauty. Take a good look around your home: I'm sure you will find some glass containers to repurpose into charming terrarium displays. Some of my favorite household items to use include mason jars, wine glasses, an old coffeepot, vases, and glass bottles. Terrarium purists will shake their heads and tell you that acrylic vessels are taboo. However, if you find an open vessel with good airflow and a watertight bottom, you can certainly turn it into a place for plants.

WHERE TO SHOP

If you're looking for something distinctive you will find an excellent collection of glass containers at stores like IKEA, West Elm, World Market, HomeGoods, and Michael's craft stores. For the more adventurous, acrylic containers are another medium to consider. Antique shops and thrift stores are gold mines when it comes to finding unique glassware. But steer clear of colored glass. While I love to collect it, I wouldn't put my plants in colored glass because they would have a hard time registering the right spectrum of sunlight they need to grow.

PRACTICAL VESSELS FOR YOUR PLANT SPECIES

Cacti, succulents, and air plants need good airflow. On occasion, you may see these plants in closed containers for décor purposes. However, this is not a practical solution for an extended period. Vessels with an opening or no walls at all are your best options.

Tropical plants, mosses, and ferns enjoy the high-humidity environment of a closed vessel. But some species can thrive in open containers as well.

HEADROOM

When considering a small vessel for a mini terrarium, keep in mind that all plants need room to grow. The last thing you want to do is cram plants into a space they will outgrow in a week.

Airflow is important to succulents.

RECOMMENDED TERRARIUM VESSELS

Geometric. These vessels are very popular and give off a modern vibe. Slow-growing cacti and succulents work best in these vessels. Haworthias are my favorites to plant in this type of vessel.

Cube. You can have fun adding colorful layers of sand or rocks to a vessel like this. Great for succulents, cacti, and tropical plants that do not require high humidity.

Fishbowl. A classic terrarium vessel, easy to source from any pet store.

Coffeepot. Raid the kitchen for unused glassware! A coffeepot can make a nice home for ferns and mosses.

Apothecary jar. An old favorite, it's easy to imagine ferns in this type of vessel. Tropical plants and mosses will also love this closed environment.

Bottle. Not very wide but does provide some headroom. Appropriate for mini marimo balls, small ferns, and mosses.

Cloche. An elegant vessel ready to show off your next orchid display.

Low bowl. A wide dish with lots of room for succulents and cacti to grow.

Hanging globe. This sleek modern vessel can fit pretty much anywhere. The perfect perch for an air plant or small succulent display.

BEFORE YOU BEGIN ANY TERRARIUM PROJECT

Wash your empty vessel(s) of choice in warm soapy water, inside and out, rinse, and let dry completely. The same goes for rocks and other decorative projects you intend to place inside your terrariums.

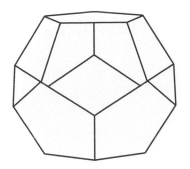

geometric

cube

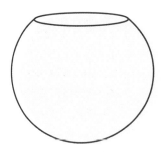

fishbowl

coffeepot

apothecary jar

bottle

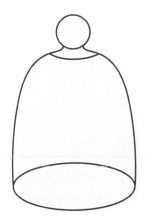

cloche

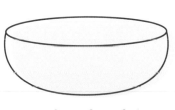

low bowl

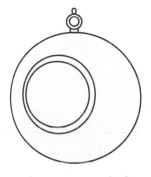

hanging globe

TERRARIUM PLANTS

THE STARS OF THE SHOW

Your vessel (open or closed) and lighting conditions will ultimately determine the types of plants you can use in your terrarium display. Most terrarium vessels can only contain smaller plant varieties. For this reason, it's important to purchase plants that are small and will grow slowly. I suggest buying succulents in plug trays, or in pots that are no larger than 2 inches (5 cm) in diameter. You can also ask your local nursery expert if they carry dwarf varieties. Of course, with a little time and patience, you can also grow your own. Check out propagation on page 235.

It's important to purchase plants that are small and will grow slowly.

INSPECT PLANTS BEFORE PURCHASING

Diseases and bugs can spread like wildfire inside a terrarium. Keep this in mind before adding any new plant to your collection. Before purchasing plants, thoroughly inspect them for any warning signs. Check the soil around the stem and the undersides of leaves for any bugs. If the leaves look scarred, wilted, or discolored in any way this could be a sign of neglect or disease. Nursing an unhealthy plant can sometimes be an uphill battle, so it's best to start off your terrarium at its best.

WHERE TO SHOP FOR TERRARIUM PLANTS

Start with your local nursery or garden center, and don't be shy about asking for recommendations. If they don't have what you are looking for, they will be more than happy to order it for you. Some pet stores and aquarium stores carry tropical plants and other specialty terrarium supplies.

HOW TO SHOP FOR PLANTS ONLINE

If I had to guess, I would say 70% of my plant collection comes from online stores and wholesalers. It may sound like a bit of a gamble because you can't physically inspect plants before you buy them, but there are a lot of reputable online stores these days. I'm thorough when researching an online retailer, and once I find one I like, I'm a loyal customer. Here are my best tips for ordering plants online:

- If possible, find a wholesale distributor within a few hundred miles of your location. The longer the ride, the higher the chance of something going wrong with your live plant shipment.

- In case of disease or damage, look for a quality guarantee policy and return policy.

- Read through customer reviews. If the reviews are mostly positive in recent months you may have a winner! Pay special attention to reviews that include pictures of the condition of plants upon arrival and unboxing.

- If it's wintertime and the plant will travel through frost, make sure a heat pack is included in the shipment to keep plants from freezing.

- Order in bulk and get free shipping!

- Make sure the plants will fit in your glass vessel before purchasing.

- Order succulents in plug trays and plants in 2 in. (5 cm) pots or smaller.

- It also doesn't hurt to talk to your mail carrier, and ask him to kindly place any live plant shipments in front of your door.

AIR PLANTS

Tillandsias, or "air plants" as they are more commonly called, belong to the Bromeliaceae (bromeliads) family. With over 500 distinct species, they come in a variety of shapes, sizes, colors, and textures. Tillandsias are native to the forests, deserts, and mountains of the Americas. In parts of the southeastern United States, where the climate is mostly sunny and humid, you'll find *Tillandsia usneoides* (Spanish moss) cascading over withering branches of old oak trees. In the deserts and tropical forests of Central and South America, you'll find incredible species of *Tillandsia* clinging to trees and rocks while happily sunbathing and drinking in the morning dew.

Tillandsias are considered *epiphytes,* meaning they use their leaves instead of roots to take in water and nutrients from the air. Unlike ordinary plants, tillandsias can survive just fine without soil—hence the name "air plant." In their natural habitat, they use their roots to anchor themselves to tall trees where they can be closer to the sunlight and have better airflow around their leaves.

Air plants sport *trichomes* (that cute peach fuzz you see on their leaves) to collect water and nutrients. Trichomes also help protect them from insects and shield them from intense sunlight. Think of it as a natural sunscreen: the more trichomes you can see on an air plant, the higher the SPF and the more it can tolerate intense sunlight.

XERIC AND MESIC

Tillandsias can be classified as two distinct groups, *xeric* and *mesic.* Xeric (from the Greek word for "dry") tillandsias are native to desert climates. *Tillandsia xerographica* has flat pale green leaves to catch as much direct sunlight as possible. Xeric varieties are popular at garden centers because they are drought tolerant and will easily survive if you forget to water them for a bit or go on vacation for a couple of weeks.

Mesic tillandsias are native to tropical climates and insist on being kept hydrated. Many varieties are bright green in appearance and have tight leaf formations.

LIGHT

Direct sunlight. Xeric tillandsias live in desert climates and require light all day. Place in direct sunlight or near a south-facing window where they can sunbathe.

Bright indirect sunlight. Mesic tillandsias do best in bright indirect sunlight. However, avoid placing them directly in a window where the glass can magnify the sunlight and scorch their leaves.

Fluorescent lighting. Most tillandsias can live in an office environment with bright overhead office lighting, making them popular desk companions.

WATERING

Upon purchasing an air plant and bringing it home, soak it to reduce its stress reaction

to its new environment. It's also important to acknowledge that air plants like their water *au naturel.* Tillandsias are sensitive to minerals (and other not-so-natural stuff) found in most tap water. To avoid toxic exposure, fill a large jar or bowl with tap water and let it sit for 24 hours. This will allow any harmful substances to evaporate. When it rains, I like to put a bucket out on my balcony and collect fresh water for my plants, but distilled water from your local store works just as well. Always allow water to reach room temperature before watering. When it comes to watering tillandsias, people usually fall into one of two camps: misting or soaking. However, a healthy combination of both is ideal for optimal air plant care.

Soaking. Your air plants should go for a swim once a week, or twice a week when the weather turns warm or if you live in a hot and dry climate. Fully submerge air plants in a bowl of water (or your kitchen sink if you have a whole tribe) for 20 to 30 minutes (see previous page). Once bath time is up, pluck them out of the water and give them a few gentle shakes to dislodge any water from their bases. Place them upside down on a paper towel or dish rack to allow the excess water to drip away. Only return air plants to their terrarium once they are completely dry (usually after a couple of hours).

Misting. Mist air plants a couple times a week with a spray bottle, or daily if you live in a dry climate. This helps keep them hydrated between soakings. When misting,

target only the leaves and do not allow water to run into the base of the plant and stay there. This could lead to rot, so it's important to work out any excess water from the base. If your air plants are part of an intricate display and too cumbersome to remove, lightly mist them every day or two.

TEMPERATURE AND HUMIDITY

Generally, tillandsias respond well to temperatures between 65 and 85 degrees Fahrenheit (18 and 30 degrees Celsius). The key to raising healthy tillandsias is to provide them with the right balance of light, water, and, for some varieties, humidity. Air-conditioning in the summer and heaters in the winter can dry the air in our homes and quickly dehydrate the more tropical varieties.

A terrarium can be the perfect home for an air plant because the walls of the vessel help to hold the humidity inside. Another great place to keep air plants is in the bathroom. While you shower, they will soak up the water vapor from the air. You get clean, they get hydrated, and everyone is happy!

FOUNDATION

One of the reasons I love tillandsias is because they don't require any soil. Their foundation is whatever you can dream up. Place them on top of rocks or sand, or hot-glue their bases to moss or wood. You can even tie a piece of twine or wire to the base of a plant and suspend it from a wall nail or ceiling hook. The sky's the limit!

FLOWERS

It might be surprising to learn that tillandsias only bloom once during their life cycle. It marks the beginning of their reproductive cycle. Blooms will shoot out from the center of the plants and sometimes flowers can last up to several weeks. Larger plants such as *Tillandsia xerographica* can bloom for months! Personally, my favorite blooms are the purple and pink flowers produced by *Tillandsia araujei* 'Purple Star' (check out plant identification on pages 40 and 41).

Blooming. If you would like to see your tillandsias bloom, they will need ideal watering and light conditions to grow to maturity. Fertilizer is not necessary but can help with blooming. Organic air plant fertilizers are readily available from air plant suppliers online. Spray the fertilizer according to the supplier's label.

Offsets. Once the blooms have lost their luster and begin to wilt, take sharp shears and snip off the blooms closest to the base. This will encourage the growth of offsets, or "pups," as they are called in the air plant world. Air plants produce one to three pups at their bases, where the roots grow. Once the pups are about one-third the size of the mother plant, you can soak the plant and then gently remove the pups so they can live on their own.

PRUNING

I admit I was a little scared to prune my first tillandsia for fear I would hurt it. But once I saw how it encouraged new growth, I was all over it! New growth springs from the centers of the air plants, which means you can prune the outer leaves to promote new growth and redirect energy to where the plants need it most. Use sharp shears to cut away old blooms, but you can gently tear away any yellow or dried leaves. Tillandsias do not need roots to collect nutrients, so, for the sake of appearances, it's okay to peel away any unsightly roots.

PROBLEMS

Leaving water between their leaves for too long or keeping them in a damp place can lead to rot and disease. This happens when too much moisture accumulates at the base of the plant (closest to the root) and encourages bacteria and fungus to grow. If you find your plants' roots turning brown, foliage becoming soft, and leaves falling off, they have most likely succumbed to root rot. I'm just going to give it to you straight up: the chance of a tillandsia surviving long term with root rot is slim, so don't get too trigger-happy with that misting bottle!

Tillandsia xerographica This "queen of tillandsias," as she is more commonly called, lives in the arid deserts of southern Mexico and Central America. In her native desert she drinks in the morning dew, so an occasional morning misting is a welcome treat. This species prefers direct sunlight but can live near a bright south-facing window in your home. If she's thirsty you will know it! If you see her leaves begin to curl you know it's time for a soak.

Tillandsia ionantha scaposa Native to Mexico and Guatemala, this species thrives in hot and humid environments. Known for their spiky green and compact foliage, they will grow dark silvery leaves in ample sunlight or dark green in shade. These are easy to display and glue to any number of objects. Mist them daily in dry climates.

Tillandsia Houston A cross between a _T. stricta_ and _T. recurvifolia_ with silvery leaves and violet highlighted tips. This rosette-shaped air plant shoots off spectacular pink blooms.

Tillandsia bulbosa Belize Native to Belize, these exotic lovelies have shiny green arms, giving them a distinct, fun appearance.

Tillandsia filifolia From Central Mexico all the way to Costa Rica this tillandsia prefers cooler temperatures and indirect sunlight. Air circulation is key to keeping this air plant happy.

Tillandsia harrisii Native to Guatemala, its velvety silver-green leaves love bright sunlight. Its dazzling red and purple blooms make it a favorite for terrarium displays.

Tillandsia araujei 'Purple Star' Known for its spiky dark green leaves and lovely purple highlights. Its name comes from a river in Brazil where it grows on rocks and foliage.

Tillandsia caput-medusae Don't worry, she won't turn you into stone, but her snakelike leaves are reminiscent of her namesake from Greek mythology. A unique air plant from Central America, she's outspoken and will tell you when she is thirsty. Her leaves will curl and then straighten again once she's been watered.

Tillandsia brachycaulos × abdita A lovely addition to any terrarium, this air plant starts off with soft green leaves that blush a deep red when they bloom.

Tillandsia xerographica

Tillandsia ionantha scaposa

Tillandsia Houston

Tillandsia bulbosa Belize

Tillandsia filifolia

Tillandsia harrisii

Tillandsia araujei
'Purple Star'

Tillandsia caput-medusae

*Tillandsia
brachycaulos × abdita*

CACTI AND SUCCULENTS

SUCCULENTS

Drought-resistant plants that are adapted to store water in their fleshy stems and leaves are called *succulents*. I like to think of them as the ultimate survivors of the plant kingdom. Most succulents are easy to propagate, and some are nearly impossible to kill—all hail the zebra plant (*Haworthia attenuata*)! Though we think of them as desert plants, they are incredibly diverse and can be found living in grasslands, rainforests, and even woodland environments. Some succulents such as lithops even have special characteristics that help them disappear into their surroundings. Native to South Africa, lithops propagate in sandy areas where only their stone-like tops are visible through the sand, hence their moniker, "living stones." Other succulents like the beloved panda plant (*Kalanchoe tomentosa*) are cute, fuzzy, and velvety to the touch (a real children's favorite).

CACTI

Did you know that cacti are succulents, too? If you're not sure what you have on your hands, *aeriols* serve as the most obvious identifying feature of a cactus. Aeriols are small round nodes that shoot out flowers and spines. There are many different kinds of spines, but the ones to really look out for all the fishhooks, which will latch onto your skin in a heartbeat! Cactus spines help keep predators away from their water storage but also serve to collect water (in the form of morning dew) and drop it onto the soil for their roots to absorb.

LIGHT

It's a bitter pill to swallow, but the reality is that succulents are designed to grow outdoors. Growing succulents indoors can be challenging, which is why it's important to provide as much sunlight as possible (some varieties can handle direct sunlight better than others). Most succulents require a minimum of 4 to 6 hours of sunlight each day. A couple hours of direct sun in the morning and filtered sun in the afternoon is ideal. Succulents do well near south- and west-facing windows, which provide the most amount of sunlight throughout the year (in the northern hemisphere).

Etiolation. When succulents do not receive enough light, they stretch and grow long until they are nearly unrecognizable from their original appearance. Echeverias are especially susceptible to this condition. They will grow out of their pretty rosette shape and develop thin, stalky stems.

Grow lights. If your succulents show signs of insufficient light or you live in an area where the winters are long and harsh, you may want to supplement lighting conditions with grow lights. There are tons of choices when it comes to artificial lighting, but I suggest buying bulbs labeled "full spectrum." Plants need a period of rest,

Cacti and succulents live harmoniously side by side.

so use a cycle of 12 hours on, 12 hours off for best results. Grow lights are available from online garden-supply stores and stores that specialize in hydroponics.

Low-light succulents. If your space does not allow for a bright light source or grow lights, not to worry—there is still hope! A majority of haworthias and gasterias will do just fine in low-light conditions.

WATERING

It's always better to underwater succulents than to overwater them. It's also important to let the soil dry out completely between waterings to avoid root rot. On the other hand, waiting too long can cause the soil to compact, and the roots will lose their ability to uptake water. Watering is dependent on the container size, type of plant, climate, and time of year. Generally, watering succulents every 10 to 14 days during the growing months (March to October) and once

every three weeks to one month during the colder months (November to April) will suffice. The only exception to this is that cacti don't need to be watered at all when they go dormant in the winter months. They are designed to conserve their energy when there is not enough sun for them to grow, so don't feel too badly about not watering them in the winter.

Contrary to popular belief, dried leaves are not a good indicator that your succulents need a drink. Succulents produce new growth from the center of the plants. The presence of dried and dying leaves on the outside of the succulent is normal; this makes room for new leaves, so don't be fooled and run the risk of overwatering.

Household tap water can contain salt, chlorine, and other minerals that can leave a chalky white residue on leaves. To avoid this, use rainwater or distilled water, or let the tap water sit in a watering can for 24 hours

The narrow nozzle of a plastic syringe helps direct water to only the base of the plant.

before use. Always allow soil to dry out completely before watering.

How to water. I suggest watering succulents inside a terrarium with a plastic syringe or squeeze bottle with a narrow nozzle and clearly marked measurements. The nozzle helps direct water to only the base of the plant and helps avoid drenching the entire display. This is especially helpful if your scene includes sand art. I strongly advise against using large watering cans, or you may accidently overwater.

Signs of overwatering. Soggy, translucent, or yellowing leaves are generally a good indicator of overwatering. Echeverias are especially sensitive to overwatering and will begin to show these symptoms within a few days.

Signs of underwatering. Symptoms of underwatering include shriveling, puckered leaves and visible aerial roots. These roots branch out from the stem of the succulent far away from the soil, which is the succulent's way of searching out and collecting moisture from the air.

TEMPERATURE AND HUMIDITY

Some species are native to harsh, cold climates and can survive freezing temperatures (way to go guys!). These hardy succulents are usually best suited for outdoors. On average, succulents and cacti best suited for terrariums need minimum temperatures of 40 to 50 degrees Fahrenheit (5 to 10 degrees Celsius). During the day, temperatures between 70 and 85 degrees Fahrenheit (21 and 30 degrees Celsius) will keep your succulents warm and cozy.

FOUNDATION

Always use a soil mix specifically formulated for cacti and succulents. There is truly nothing sadder than to watch a cactus succumb to root rot. For a time, it looks a little dull, then a little slouchy, until it eventually collapses in on itself in a sorry, soggy mess. While overwatering is first to blame, don't discount the vital role soil can play in preventing such a tragic end. Commercial soil mix from any garden center is perfectly acceptable to use in terrariums.

PRUNING

When pruning succulents, it's important to use clean, sharp shears or scissors. This will help prevent bacteria from entering the stem. Dodge the risk of fungus or root rot by allowing the cut to dry and callus over before watering.

Pruning is necessary when the succulent:

- Begins leaning to one side due to etiolation (stretching).
- Begins outgrowing the terrarium vessel.
- Shows signs of disease or rot. Depending on the species, saving some of the leaves for propagation or cutting a part of the plant to pot may be an option.
- Begins to die after growing offspring.

PROBLEMS

Overwatering succulents can lead to soggy roots and root rot. Not only will this kill the plant, it could also attract pests. Read more on how to handle pests on page 232.

Pachyphytum **Moon Silver** Identifiable by their plump and tubular leaves, their colors range from green to hues of purple. Be careful not to overwater. In fact, it's better to underwater this one.

Opuntia rufida minima **Cinnamon Cactus** With their pads covered in cinnamon-colored spines, these miniature cacti are also known as "prickly pears."

Graptopetalum amethystinum **Lavender Pebbles** Bright colors with a milky coating give these succulents their unique appearance.

Aloe zanzibarica **Zanzibar Aloe** These have elongated leaves that are green with white, bumpy spots covering the surface as they grow in outward rosettes.

Lithops **spp. Living Stones** As their name implies, these look like pebbles, and they evolved this way to avoid being eaten by prey. This plant is a fun addition to any desert terrarium.

Sedum rubrotinctum **'Aurora' Pink Jelly Bean** These have small, plump, tubular leaves that have different shades of green and pink. They make great propagation plants!

Gymnocalycium mihanovichii **Moon Cactus** These cacti come in a variety of colors. Man-made creations, the top halves are grafted to the bodies of cacti to keep their pretty colors alive and vibrant.

Adromischus cristatus **Crinkle Leaf Plant** Native to South Africa, this succulent is full of personality and loved for its drought resistance.

Echeveria **'Devotion Petite'** These grow in a cluster, and their fiery, velvet-red leaves are a total showstopper.

Pachyphytum
Moon Silver

Opuntia rufiada minima
Cinnamon Cactus

Graptopetalum amethystinum
Lavender Pebbles

Aloe Zanzibarica
Zanzibar Aloe

Lithops spp.
Living Stones

Sedum rubrotinctum
'Aurora' Pink Jelly Bean

Gymnocalycium mihanovichii
Moon Cactus

Adromischus cristatus
Crinkle Leaf Plant

Echeveria
'Devotion Petite'

Crassula ovata 'Gollum' **Jade Plant** This is a small, shrubby green succulent with a reddish tint on the ends of its cylindrical leaves. Just wait until you see its star-shaped white flowers.

Crassula rupestris This species typically grows in clusters and has thickly stacked green leaves that are ovate in shape. It is fantastic in containers.

Euphorbia mammillaris **Indian Corn Cob** This one has a thick corn cob-shaped stem with spiky spines. It blooms yellow *cyathium* (little false flowers) on the tips of each stem in the winter and summer.

Graptosedum 'Darley Sunshine' This one is a hybrid succulent that loves partial shade. Its thick green leaves have pinkish tips that form a tight rosette. Be sure not to overwater as it can cause root rot.

Pachyveria 'Clavifolia' **Jeweled Crown** This jewel of a succulent has thick green leaves with pinkish tips that grow in an up-curved pattern that forms a tight rosette. It maintains this shape while young and settles with age. Orange and red flowers bloom in spring and summer. It is perfect for containers.

Echeveria prolifica This has small green leaves with pinkish tips that resemble a rosette pattern. It is perfect for terrariums and floral arrangements.

Echeveria 'Perle von Nurnberg' This has beautiful pinks and purples with an exquisite leaf shape that makes up a rosette pattern. It blooms brightly colored flowers in summer.

Haworthia fasciata Its succulent leaves, arranged in a rosette, have white tubercles along their short, tapered leaves. It is often referred to as the zebra plant.

Sedum adolphii 'Golden Glow' This one has thick green leaves with pinkish tips that form a tight rosette cluster. True to its name, this species has a golden hue to them.

Crasulla ovata
'Gollum' Jade Plant

Crassula rupestris

Euphorbia mammillaris
Indian Corn Cob

Graptosedum
'Darley Sunshine'

Pachyveria 'Clavifolia'
Jeweled Crown

Echeveria prolifica

Echeveria
'Perle von Nurnberg'

Haworthia fasciata

Sedum adolphii
'Golden Glow'

MOSSES

Throughout history, mosses have been used for their various medicinal and antiseptic properties. During World War I, soldiers were bandaged with bits of sphagnum moss to help keep infections at bay. It can also be used to treat several common skin ailments such as eczema and psoriasis, insect bites, and even burns.

There are around 12,000 types of moss scattered around the world, all of them deriving from the Bryophyta family of plants. They come in all different shades of greens, textures, and sizes. Unlike other terrarium plants, mosses have no vascular system. In other words, they do not have tissues that transport water from the roots and deliver nutrients to different parts of the plant. Instead of roots, they have modest hairlike structures called *rhizoids* that cling to soil for stability.

LIGHT
Most mosses are native to woodlands and forests where the environment is either shaded or sunlight is filtered through the trees.

WATERING
Watering depends on the type of moss. Generally, it's important to keep the soil moist at all times and to mist to keep the foliage green. Do not allow the soil to get soggy or to dry out completely.

TEMPERATURE AND HUMIDITY
Most mosses benefit from the warm humidity inside a closed terrarium. If you

are going to plant live mosses inside an open terrarium, it's best to a pair with other tropical plants to create a mini ecosystem of humidity lovers.

FOUNDATION

Mosses like their soil slightly on the acidic side, so peat moss is an excellent soil medium for all mosses. Because mossariums are prone to mold, the acidity of peat moss will help prevent mold from growing in your terrarium, or at least control the problem until you can intervene and remove the mold. However, that is not to say they can't be planted in regular potting soil, especially if paired with tropical plants.

PRUNING

Pruning may be necessary when your moss begins to outgrow its vessel. Trim with clean and sharp shears as needed.

PROBLEM

Mold grows in response to overwatering. It's a common problem with mossariums and, if left unchecked, can spread like wildfire. If you find fuzzy gray filaments inside your terrarium, the first order of business is to remove the problem. Use a cotton swab to wipe away any mold you see. Then you can try rebalancing the ecosystem by leaving the terrarium open for a few days. This will allow excess water to evaporate and stop any new mold growth dead in its tracks. If mold continues to grow in a spot, you will need to swap it out with a fresh replacement. Cut away the troublesome area with sharp shears or a knife and replace with new moss.

Preserved Sheet Moss Available at most craft stores and floral supply stores, this carpet of greenery requires no maintenance.

Leucobryum glaucum **Pincushion Moss** Growing in green, jewellike mounds, this species is happiest in low-light conditions.

Preserved Reindeer Moss Called "reindeer moss" because it's a favorite snack for reindeer. It's really a species of lichen. This colorful preserved type needs no maintenance.

Dried Sphagnum Moss Used as a separation layer for terrariums, dried sphagnum moss can be purchased in bales online or from your local pet store. It comes in a light straw-like color and, after soaking in water for a few minutes, it turns a dark amber color. Once you ring out the excess water it is ready to use in a terrarium.

Fruticose Lichen Another moss impostor, this little green mound is actually a lichen fungus.

Tillandsia usneoides **Spanish Moss** Not exactly a moss as the name implies; in actuality it's an air plant that has been preserved and is used as a decorative accent in terrariums.

Selaginella **spp. Spike Moss** More of a fern than a moss, it provides beautiful ground cover in a tropical plant terrarium.

Hypnum cupressiforme **Hypnum Moss** This species grows low to the ground and can be found growing all over the world in the most unexpected places. It's a true adventurer!

Dicranum scoparium **Mood Moss** This is a popular moss in terrarium designs. Soak it in water for a bit to bring it back to life and mist weekly to keep it green and vibrant.

Preserved Sheet Moss

Leucobryum glaucum
Pincushion Moss

Preserved Reindeer Moss

Dried Sphagnum Moss

Fruticose Lichen

Tillandsia usneoides
Spanish Moss

Selaginella spp.
Spike Moss

Hypnum cupressiforme
Hypnum Moss

Dicranum scoparium
Mood Moss

TROPICAL PLANTS

My sentiment has always been that tropical plants can make small spaces feel bright and full of life. Tropical plants come in many different sizes, leaf structures, colors, and textures. Most are native to tropical and subtropical rainforests, where they live under large canopies of overlapping tree branches, on the forest floor, where only dappled sunlight reaches them. Fortunately for us, the filtered light inside our homes makes them well suited for life indoors.

Many of these plants are already familiar to us as regular houseplants—ferns, ivy, and palms, for example. Ferns have been around for millions of years and have adapted to live in a diverse range of environments including marshes in Florida and deserts in Arizona. Most ferns flourish in the high humidity that terrariums provide. But always be sure to read the label on the plant pot to determine the best conditions for your fern. The key to selecting tropical fern varieties is to look for something small and slow growing.

LIGHT

Generally, tropical plants prefer bright, filtered light. Depending on the species, some ferns and palms will do well in low-light environments. Occasionally rotate your terrarium to avoid plants leaning in one direction toward a light source. These plants are sensitive to climate fluctuations and do best when light, water, and temperature are all balanced.

WATERING

Tropical plants require much more moisture than other terrarium plants to thrive. For a closed vessel, you may need to open the top every few months to prune and clean up dried leaves. Check the soil for moisture and add a little extra water if necessary. For open vessels, add a few ounces of water about every three days. If the leaves begin to wilt, this is an indication that more water is necessary. Tropical plants will show signs of underwatering within days.

TEMPERATURE AND HUMIDITY

Most tropical plants prefer average temperatures between 50 and 85 degrees Fahrenheit (10 to 30 degrees Celsius) and slightly cooler temperatures at night. Since these plants are native to humid climates, they do very well in a closed container or with high glass walls. To keep the humidity level up and make your plants feel right at home, do not allow the soil to dry out completely between waterings.

FOUNDATION

The soil mix you use depends on the type of plants in the terrarium. For orchids, orchid soil mix, bark, or just sphagnum moss works fine. African violets require a more acidic formula and have their own type of potting

mix. In general, tropical plants do fine with regular commercial potting mix. I stay away from potting mixes enriched with organic bug castings or those that promise moisture control; none of this is necessary for a small terrarium display.

PRUNING

Tropical plants grow much faster than succulents and air plants. Pruning ferns and leafy plants is essential in encouraging fullness rather than height. With all plants, use clean and sharp scissors or shears to avoid diseases attacking the stem. Make a clean cut just above where the leaf or branch is attached. If you are using an airtight vessel, you may need to open the vessel to prune the plants or clean up some dried leaves every three months or so.

PROBLEMS

Tropical plants are very sensitive to our living conditions and sometimes need an adjustment period to acclimate to their new environment. Getting tropical plants into a terrarium as soon as you get them home can help. But even then, you may run into some problems.

Brown leaves. This could be due to temperature fluctuations, underwatering, or too much sunlight. Move the terrarium to a shadier area of your home, check the soil for moisture, and keep away from air vents or heaters. Prune away any brown leaves to allow for new growth.

Yellow leaves. This is a tricky one. Either too much moisture or too little moisture could be to blame. The water is either evaporating too quickly or not at all, depending on where the terrarium is in your home. If there is too much condensation in the terrarium, crack open the lid just a bit to release some moisture.

Wilting leaves. This is most likely due to lack of moisture and/or the sun overheating the plant. If there is not enough water being pulled up through the plant to the leaves, then there is nothing supporting the leaves to stay upright. Water the plants in the morning and move to a shadier area of your home until it bounces back.

***Adiantum raddianum* Delta Maidenhair Fern** This feathery frond friend is a diva in disguise. This plant can only thrive in high humidity. Place in a closed terrarium away from direct sunlight, and prune when necessary.

***Chamaedorea elegans* Parlor Palm** This regal fern made popular during the Victorian era does well in low-light conditions. It prefers temperatures between 65 and 80 degrees Fahrenheit (18 and 27 degrees Celsius). Prone to brown leaf tips when air and soil are left dry for too long.

***Nephrolepis cordifolia* 'Duffii' Lemon Button Fern** With leaves resembling a fishbone, and tolerant of low light, this plant is relatively drought tolerant. However, to keep it in tip-top health, avoid letting the soil dry out completely.

***Fittonia albivenis* Nerve Plant** Native to the rainforests of South America, its mesmerizing mosaic-like foliage is a popular variety with terrarium designers. Instead of adding a topdressing layer to your terrarium, plant this instead. It spreads as it grows to create ground cover. Look out for wilted leaves—it's telling you it's thirsty.

***Saintpaulia* African Violet** Native to the humid mountain regions of East Africa, this common houseplant does very well indoors. For closed terrariums, it is important to occasionally leave the lid open to provide some air circulation and to prevent mold growing on the leaves. It prefers African violet soil mix to regular potting mix.

***Polystichum tsus-simense* Korean Rock Fern** These dark green fronds enjoy low-light conditions and make excellent ground cover— eventually, you'll have a fern carpet inside your terrarium.

***Asparagus densiflorus* 'Sprengeri' Asparagus Fern** Leaves resembling miniature trees makes this fern the perfect terrarium plant. In shade, its foliage is dark green; in the sun, its foliage turns light green. A little sun in the morning followed by shade in the afternoon will keep her happy.

***Hypoestes phyllostachya* 'Rose Splash' Polka Dot Plant** This beautiful little plant loves the terrarium life. It's small and full, but if left unchecked it could get leggy and lose its adorable fullness. Prune leaves to keep it small and provide plenty of filtered light. Keep the soil moist.

***Syngonium* 'Berry Allusion'** Native to Central and South America, with leaves shaped like arrowheads, this plant prefers bright filtered light, high humidity, and temperatures between 60 and 80 degrees Fahrenheit (15 and 27 degrees Celsius).

Adiantum raddianum
Delta Maidenhair Fern

Chamaedorea elegans
Parlor Palm

Nephrolepis cordifolia
'Duffii' Lemon Button Fern

Fittonia albivenis
Nerve Plant

Saintpaulia
African Violet

Polystichum tsus-simense
Korean Rock Fern

Asparagus densiflorus
'Sprengeri' Asparagus Fern

Hypoestes phyllostachya
'Rose Splash' Polka Dot Plant

Syngonium
'Berry Allusion'

FOUNDATION

THAT WHICH LIES BENEATH

Now that we have selected a vessel and picked out our favorite plants, we need to consider the layer that will be the foundation for our landscape. On pages 16–21, we saw how the foundation is divided into four distinct layers, each of which serves a specific purpose, and how they all work together to keep a terrarium's ecosystem nourished and healthy.

Soil provides a medium for roots to anchor themselves to the ground and keep the plant upright. It also absorbs water long enough for the roots to take it in and distribute it to other parts of the plant. While plants make their own food through the process of photosynthesis, they need nutrients from the soil such as magnesium, nitrogen, and phosphorus to grow and stay healthy. Soil mixes come in different varieties. There are specific mixes for succulents, cacti, palms, orchids, and African violets.

DIY SUCCULENT MIX

If you already have potting soil and want to try your hand at making your own succulent soil mix, try this basic recipe.

In a medium-sized bowl, mix together:
- 3 parts potting soil
- 2 parts horticultural sand
- 1 part perlite

You might also consider adding pine bark, granite, or coconut husk (coir) to further improve drainage.

The soil top layer is very important for the root system.

Peat moss mix is best for mosses and plants that prefer slightly acidic soil. It consists of decayed sphagnum moss harvested from wetlands. Sphagnum moss is often skimmed off the top of bogs, and then the bogs are drained to collect the peat moss below. The sediment is then screened, dried, and sold to garden stores in bags or brick bales. Peat moss can hold a tremendous amount of moisture, which makes it an excellent soil medium for mossariums (terrariums exclusively featuring live mosses). The acidic quality of the soil can help prevent the growth of bacteria and mold.

Orchid mix consists of a coarse blend of peat moss, perlite, and fig bark. Unlike most tropical plants, orchids do not need soil to grow, but their roots need the perfect amount of moisture. Phalaenopses (commonly found in garden stores) do not like soggy roots but hate being left to dry out completely. Adding a thin layer of orchid potting mix or even just the bark will allow excess water to run off easily while retaining moisture.

Potting soil mix is suitable for most tropical plant terrariums. Generally, it's a mix of peat moss, pine bark, perlite, and vermiculite. Perlite and vermiculite are both additives that are volcanic in origin. They help lighten the soil and provide oxygen to the roots. If the soil were too dense, it would compact on the roots, and the roots would lose the ability to take in water. Commercial potting mixes work just fine for terrariums. You may want to look for "soilless" on the label. Stay away from garden soil, which contains extra additives that are better suited for outdoor gardening than indoor.

African violet mix is made especially for this species. African violets (*Saintpaulia*) need slightly acidic soil (pH between 5.8 and 6.2) for their dainty roots to absorb nutrients. Their roots are also prone to collapse when the soil is too dense for their liking. African violet potting soil contains no soil at all, just peat moss and a lightening additive such as perlite.

Cactus and succulent mix can hold moisture and nutrients but drain quickly before damaging the roots. Peat moss is the main ingredient, followed by mediums that help with drainage such as bark, sand, gravel, and perlite. The important thing is to look for a label that guarantees proper drainage for cacti and succulents.

Peat Moss

Orchid Mix

Potting Soil Mix

African Violet Mix

Cactus and Succulent Mix

DECORATIVE ELEMENTS

THE SWAG

In any living scene or landscape, the plants are always the stars of the show. But if you have a theme in mind, on occasion it doesn't hurt to add a few special touches to better tell the story. Does your scene take place in prehistoric times? Add a dinosaur. Or does it take place near the water? Add beach sand, seashells, and a starfish! These are just a few examples of small decorative touches you can add to your terrarium.

Decorative stones and pebbles. Easy to find in craft and floral supply stores, these come in a million different sizes and colors.

Preserved toppers. Naturally preserved seeds and pods can add a whimsical look. Look for cat's eye pods, bakuli pods, and eucalyptus pods.

Seashells and sand dollars. Scour the beach and bring home beach accents for your next project.

Blue crushed glass. This adds sparkle and can be used to represent water in a beach-themed terrarium.

Preserved reindeer moss. This comes in a variety of colors and really makes your terrarium pop!

Toys and miniatures. These are a great way to pique a child's interest in terrariums, plus they can tell a fun story.

Crystals. Always fun in terrarium design, my favorites include amethyst, citrine, pyrite, and rose quartz.

TOOLS OF THE TRADE

The following list is meant to give you an understanding of some essential tools used in terrarium making. You don't need anything too fancy, and some items you can make yourself. In fact one of my most-used tools, a funnel, is nothing more than a piece of rolled-up paper held together with a piece of tape. There are projects listed in this book that require additional tools; those are listed within their respective projects.

Paper or plastic funnel. This tool helps a lot with cleanly layering sand and soil. Make your own funnel out of copy paper, newspaper, or sturdy card stock. Roll it up and tape it together.

Gardening gloves. Wear these to protect your hands from soil and cactus spines.

Long spoon. This helps with adding soil and rocks in tight spaces.

Long scissors. These are perfect when working with tall vessels. Prune dead leaves and trim mosses and plants from outgrowing their vessels too quickly.

Tweezers. Long and short tweezers help with placing decorative items, moss, and plants.

Squeeze bottle with narrow nozzle. This is an absolute must when watering delicate displays. It allows you to easily water roots without getting water everywhere.

Scissors. These are useful when cutting fiberglass screen to use as a separation later, and for cutting preserved sheet moss.

Garden shears. These are used to take succulent cuttings and use them in projects.

Wine cork. Place the sharp end of a bamboo skewer halfway into a wine cork to create a flattening tool used to level sand and soil.

Bamboo skewer. Use to position decorations in tight spaces, dig a space into soil before placing your plant, or use with a wine cork to make a flattening tool.

Floral wire. This is used to hang terrariums, secure plants to projects, or as decoration on its own.

Plastic syringe. This is my favorite tool for watering. Water plants with pinpoint precision while avoiding overwatering.

Small garden trowel/mini shovel. Use this to scoop up soil and sand.

Page from magazine (or newspaper). Fold paper over several times and wrap it around cacti to position inside terrariums and avoid coming into direct contact with their prickly spines.

Hot glue gun and glue sticks (alternatively, E6000 glue). This is used to glue miniature figurines to rocks and air plants to decorative objects.

PART 2: PROJECTS

A BUDDHAFUL MEMO BOARD

USHER IN GOOD FORTUNE WHILE STAYING ON TASK

In many cultures around the world, the jade plant is considered a symbol of good things to come. In Chinese culture, shopkeepers display jade plants to attract good fortune, wealth, and prosperity. In Indian culture, the elephant is synonymous with wisdom and friendship. So it should come as no surprise that the elephant bush plant is so appropriately named because it happens to be this peaceful pachyderm's favorite snack. In this project you'll first make a modern, off-the-wall memo board. Then fill your planter with rich green moss, lucky jade plants, and a miniature Buddha for that added Zen vibe.

VESSEL
- 11 x 14 x ¼ in. (28 x 36 cm x 6 mm) acrylic/polycarbonate sheet (Lexan shatter resistant)
- 9 x 3 in. (23 x 8 cm) acrylic organizer tray

FOUNDATION
- 1 cup (240 mL) aquarium gravel (black and white mix)
- ¼ cup (60 mL) horticultural charcoal
- 1 cup (240 mL) succulent soil mix
- fiberglass screen sheet (or sphagnum moss)

PLANTS
- 1 x *Crassula ovata* 'Obliqua' Jade Plant
- 1 x *Portulacaria afra* f. *microphylla* Elephant Bush
- 1 x clump *Dicranum scoparium* Mood Moss

DECORATIVE ELEMENTS
- 1 x stone Buddha figurine
- 1 x river pebble

TOOLS AND MATERIALS
- 4 x clear adhesive glue dots
- 4 x aluminum sign standoff mounts with combination screws
- 12 x 12 in. (30.5 x 30.5 cm) white brick cardstock
- painter's tape
- acrylic cement glue
- marker
- ¼ in. (6 mm) drill bit
- screwdriver bit (or regular screwdriver)
- paper trimmer (or scissors)
- power drill
- ruler
- spoon (optional)
- tweezers (optional)
- wood scraps to protect your table surface

BEFORE YOU BEGIN

To protect your work surface, place a couple of wood scraps underneath the acrylic sheet where you will drill (trust me, you don't want to drill through your table!).

1. Mark acrylic sheet where you will drill. Use painter's tape to tape down each corner of the acrylic sheet. To measure where the standoffs will be placed, use a ruler to measure ½ in. (13 mm) from each corner. Use a marker to mark an X where they meet.

2. Drill into each corner of the acrylic sheet. With moderate speed and pressure, drill into the center of each X you have marked until you hit wood. Then set your drill to reverse and slowly pull the drill bit out. Remove the protective plastic from the acrylic sheet and set aside.

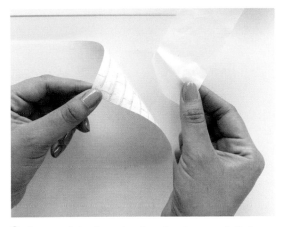

3. Cut cardstock and set as background. Cut the cardstock to 10 x 12 in. (25 x 30.5 cm) using a paper cutter or scissors. Adhere the cardstock to one side of the acrylic sheet by placing glue dots in each corner. Make sure the side with the design is facing the acrylic sheet.

4. Assemble the memo board. Add acrylic cement glue to one side of the acrylic organizer tray and adhere the tray ½ in. (13 mm) from the bottom of the acrylic sheet. Once centered, press down firmly. Follow the recommended dry time on the manufacturer's label—two hours should be enough.

5. Mount screws to wall. Position the memo board on the wall where you want it to hang. Use a pencil to mark through the holes onto the wall where you will drill. Drill combination screws where you marked the wall using a screwdriver bit (or regular screwdriver). Twist the standoff mounts into the combination screws.

7. Add drainage and filtration layers. Layer gravel inside the acrylic tray. Next, cut a piece of fiberglass screen (you can eyeball the measurements) slightly smaller than the inside of the tray. Place the fiberglass screen over the gravel and use a spoon to add horticultural charcoal on top of the screen.

6. Secure memo board with standoff mount covers. Line up the holes of the memo board with the standoff mounts and push memo board into place. Finally, twist the mount covers over the combination screws until they are completely covered.

8. Add substrate layer and plants. Place a jade plant on the left side of the tray, and an elephant bush plant on the right side of the tray. Make sure you cover the roots with soil.

9. Add moss. Separate small clumps of moss and place them over the root balls of each plant. Then position a large single piece of moss in the center. Trim off a bit of moss from the middle section where you will place the Buddha (or figurine of your choice).

10. Add decorative elements. Add a river stone in the center of the tray, in front of the moss. Place your Buddha figure on top of the stone.

TERRARIUM CARE

Use a spray bottle to water plants once a week. Mist the moss a couple times a week to keep the color looking green and vibrant.

AIR PLANT-ETARIUM

ONE GIANT LEAP FOR PLANTKIND

Growing up in Los Angeles, my favorite place to visit was the planetarium at the Griffith Park Observatory. Journeying through the universe while never leaving "home" was always a delightful experience, and one I'm sharing with you! Keeping our two feet on planet Earth, and using the cosmos as our design inspiration, we'll create gravity-defying worlds for our exotic air plants to call home. Create a set of three, or let your imagination run wild and make an entire solar system!

VESSEL
- 3 x 4 in. (10 cm) hanging glass globes

FOUNDATION
- 1½ cups (350 mL) silver decorative rocks

PLANTS
- 2 x *Tillandsia ionantha scaposa*
- 1 x *Tillandsia ionantha rubra*

DECORATIVE ELEMENTS
- preserved reindeer moss (blue, green, and pink)
- 20 gauge wire (blue, green, and pink)
- transparent monofilament cord
- for the pink globe: desert rose and rose quartz
- for the blue globe: rose quartz and blue larimar stone
- for the green globe: desert rose and raw lepidolite stone

TOOLS AND MATERIALS
- scissors or wire cutters
- craft glue
- 3 x ceiling or wall hooks

PRO TIP

Before purchasing air plants, make sure they will fit inside your glass globes without touching the glass. If the glass gets warm the leaves may scorch or dry.

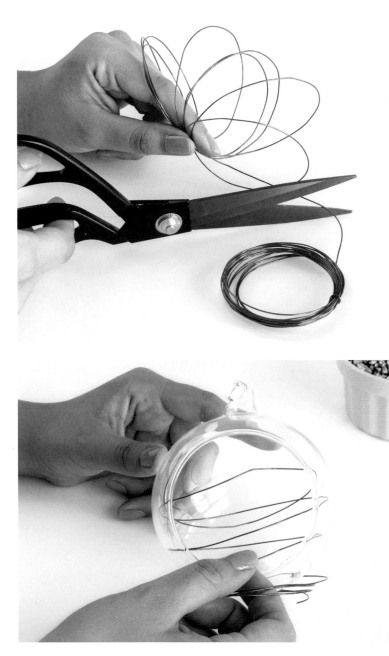

1. Cut and shape the wire.
The wire may already come in the circular shape we need. In this case, unwind 10 circles of wire (hold with one hand to keep the circular shape) and cut it with scissors. Gently stretch your wire until it is about the same circumference as the globe.

2. Insert wire into glass globe and add rocks. Insert one end of the wire into the globe and keep feeding the wire until it's all inside. Pour decorative silver rocks into the bottom of the vessel.

TERRARIUM CARE

Lightly mist your terrarium every day in the spring and summer or during hot weather, and a couple times a week in cold weather. Give air plants a quarter turn weekly to provide even sunlight on all sides.

3. Arrange moss inside the globe. Place a small piece of preserved reindeer moss near the front opening.

4. Add air plants and crystals. Place the air plants on the mosses and place two stones inside each globe. Tie monofilament cord to the terrariums and add a dab of glue to the knot (monofilament cord can loosen over time). Hang the globes from ceiling or wall hooks.

SHAKE 'N BAKE

FEELING BLUE NEVER FELT SO GOOD

A good rule of thumb is, the greener the succulent, the more suitable it is for indoor growing. Most pastel and deep-colored succulents require maximum sunlight and are at risk of stretching (etiolating) when subjected to low-light conditions indoors. But who can resist picking out pretty pastels for an indoor terrarium scene? *Kalanchoe tomentosa* and *Echeveria* 'Orion' are among my favorite pastel succulents for terrariums. They grow slowly, and a few hours of bright morning sun and placement near a bright south- or east-facing window will work just fine. If you just can't pass up the chance to snatch up a colorful succulent, I don't blame you! You can also always encourage slow growth by planting them close together in a tight yet cozy cluster.

A blue baking pan was my inspiration for this colorful living landscape. Repurposing ordinary objects from around the house is one of my favorite ways to dream up new terrarium scenes. Not to mention that secondhand stores are a gold mine when it comes to inspiration and finding unconventional vessels to transform into terrariums.

VESSEL
- 10 in. (25 cm) round blue baking pan

FOUNDATION
- 2 cups (475 mL) white rocks
- 5 cups (1.2 L) succulent soil mix
- 1 cup (240 mL) horticultural charcoal
- fiberglass screen sheet (or sphagnum moss)

PLANTS
- 1 x *Sedum rubrotinctum* Jelly Bean
- 1 x *Echeveria* 'Devotion Petite'
- 1 x *Pachyphytum* Moon Silver
- 1 x *Kalanchoe tomentosa* Panda Plant
- 3 x *Echeveria* 'Orion'
- 1 x *Echeveria* 'Violet Queen'

DECORATIVE ELEMENTS
- 1 x raw rose quartz gemstone (small)
- 1 x raw blue calcite gemstone (large)
- 2 cups (475 mL) marble and jade pebbles

TOOLS AND MATERIALS
- scissors
- bamboo skewer (optional)

1. Add rocks. Line the bottom of the baking pan with white rocks. Fill to about one-fourth of the pan's height to provide adequate drainage.

2. Filtration layer. Use scissors to cut a piece of fiberglass screen to fit inside the baking pan. It doesn't need to fit perfectly since it will not be visible. Place the screen over the white rocks. Spread a thin layer of charcoal over the screen to keep it from rolling and, of course, to help with the water filtration process.

3. Add soil and large succulents.
Fill the baking pan with succulent soil, leaving about a quarter of an inch from the rim of the pan for decorative elements. With your index finger (or a bamboo skewer), make small pockets in the soil for your succulents. Remove the largest succulents from their pots first and plant them in the scene. The tallest succulents should be planted in the back to allow the shorter ones in the front to be seen. *Pachyphylum* is a real showstopper, so I planted it in the front and diagonally from where the large calcite crystal will be placed to balance out the landscape.

4. Add smaller succulents.
Plant the little ones in the center of the pan, but leave room for the large calcite crystal in the back and a small rock garden in the front. Packing the echeverias in close proximity to one another will promote slow growth and a longer-lasting terrarium scene.

TERRARIUM CARE

Water this terrarium once a week (6 oz./180 mL) with a squeeze bottle, and water less in the cold winter months. Place it near a window in the sunniest spot in your home.

5. Add decorative elements. Use small polished rocks like jade and marble as topdressing to complement the sparkly crystals. Add a large calcite crystal between the echeverias, and a small rose quartz crystal in the mini rock garden, adjacent to the *Pachyphytum*.

SPARK YOUR CREATIVITY

Upcycle everyday objects from around your home into delightful living works of art. Candle holders, coffeepots, mixing bowls, and wine bottles are all there, just waiting to be repurposed.

BEST FRONDS FOREVER

A FOREST FANTASY FIT FOR A UNICORN!

Hidden gems are nestled between tropical plants and lush green moss. Below the surface, a kaleidoscope of rocks and sand are neatly layered. To top it all off, a blissful unicorn adds a touch of the magical to the overall presentation. Right at home in a kid's room, this project is a great hands-on activity for kids and adults alike.

VESSEL
- 10 x 6 in. (25 x 15 cm) glass vessel with cork lid

FOUNDATION
- 1½ cups (350 mL) purple aquarium gravel
- ¾ cup (180 mL) horticultural charcoal
- 1 cup (240 mL) white sand
- 1 cup (240 mL) blue sand
- 3 cups (700 mL) potting soil
- fiberglass screen sheet (or sphagnum moss)

PLANTS
- 1 x Rhizomatous *Begonia versicolor*
- 1 x *Adiantum capillus-veneris* Maidenhair Fern
- 1 x *Hypoestes phyllostachya* 'Rose Splash' Polka Dot Plant
- *Dicranum scoparium* Mood Moss

DECORATIVE ELEMENTS
- 3 x agate sliced gemstones in purple and blue
- 1 x small unicorn figurine (or figurine of choice)
- 1 x piece preserved sheet moss

TOOLS AND MATERIALS
- funnel
- flattening tool (bamboo skewer and cork)
- small natural hair brush
- long tweezers or chopsticks
- scissors
- marker
- multipurpose craft glue

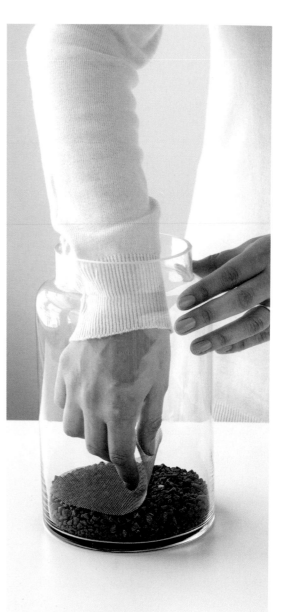

1. Add a drainage layer. Use a funnel to pour purple aquarium gravel into the container. Gently shake the container to allow the gravel to level out.

2. Add a screen layer. Place the container on a sheet of fiberglass screen and trace around the container with a marker. Cut out the fiberglass screen with scissors. Place the screen inside the container, covering the gravel. This will help with filtration and prevent sediments from falling into the bottom rock layer, which serves as a water reservoir.

3. Create a filtration layer. Pour in a layer of horticultural charcoal—enough to cover the screen mesh and keep the corners of the mesh from curling up.

4. Add a layer of soil. Funnel a thin layer of potting soil into the vessel. The soil should completely cover the charcoal layer.

5. Add decorative sand layers. Pour in a layer of white sand. Use the flattening tool to pack the sand in tight. This will create a cleaner layer when you add the next layer. Pour in a layer of blue sand and again, level out the sand with a flattening tool.

6. Add in the remaining soil. Use the skewer end of your flattening tool to make small pockets for your plants. This step also helps you decide where to best place your plants, depending on size and shape.

7. Use long tweezers or chopsticks to place plants inside the pockets of soil and cover with additional soil.

8. Carefully place moss and gemstones between plants and around the inside of the container.

TERRARIUM CARE

Use a small brush to clean off any dirt or sand from plant leaves. Wait 24 hours before the first watering to allow the plant roots to heal and settle in. Use a plastic syringe, turkey baster, or water bottle with a long nozzle to water plants at their bases to avoid splashing. Keep in mind that begonias are prone to mildew if water sits on their leaves for too long.

Keep your terrarium in a cool place, away from direct sunlight—direct sunlight on a glass container can give plants major sunburn. As your plants grow, keep them happy and healthy by trimming away any fronds or leaves that are touching the glass. Additionally, use a pair of long tweezers to pick up any dried leaves. Dead leaves left for too long in a humid environment can potentially lead to a host of problems, including fungus and mold (trust me, spare yourself). If you notice too much condensation inside the container (foggy and the plants are barely visible) remove the lid from the container for a few hours once or twice a week. This will quickly allow any excess condensation to evaporate.

FOR THE UNICORN LID

10. Glue the cut piece of moss to the top of the lid. Multipurpose craft glue works best on cork. (Note: when working with cork, hot glue does not bond as well as craft glue).

9. Place the lid on a sheet of preserved moss (moss-side down). Trace the lid with a marker and cut out the moss.

11. Dab a bit of glue on the underside of the unicorn figurine and push it down firmly on the lid. Before covering the terrarium with the lid, allow the glue to fully dry according to the label's recommendation.

CONCHARIUM

A SPE-SHELL KIND OF GARDEN

Decorating bathrooms with plants is a trend on the rise! Ferns, for their humidity-loving nature, are an obvious choice, but succulents and air plants are not far behind and are far less fussy. And if you are the type who forgets to water your plants, not to worry, you'll be instantly reminded to give your plants a drink every time you turn on the faucet or shower! If you have a bright window, turn your bathroom into a relaxing succulent oasis. This half-shell accent planter is the perfect bathroom statement piece. Fill it with succulents that bring to mind aquatic plants and sea grasses moving with the tide. Complement the scene with a selenite crystal resembling white coral. Whether on a bathroom counter, shelf, or at the foot of your bathtub, this project is a great way to bring some greenery into your bathroom space.

VESSEL
- seashell planter

FOUNDATION
- 3 cups (700 mL) river pebbles
- fiberglass screen sheet
- 2 cups (475 mL) horticultural charcoal
- succulent soil mix

PLANTS
- 1 x *Senecio rowleyanus* String of Pearls
- 1 x *Aloe zanzibarica* Zanzibar Aloe
- 1 x *Crassula ovata* 'Gollum' Jade Plant
- 1 x *Crassula arborescens undulatifolia* Ripple Jade
- 1 x *Senecio serpens* Blue Chalksticks
- 1 x *Tillandsia bulbosa* Belize

DECORATIVE ELEMENTS
- 1 cup (240 mL) white sand
- natural crushed shell fragments
- decorative crushed glass (turquoise)
- selenite crystal

TOOLS AND MATERIALS
- bamboo skewer
- scissors

From left to right—*Crassula ovata, Senecio serpens, Crassula arborescens undulatifolia, Aloe zanzibarica, Tillandsia bulbosa, Senecio rowleyanus*

1. Add a drainage layer. Add rocks to the bottom of your seashell planter. Fill to about 1 in. (2.5 cm) high.

2. Create a filtration layer. Roughly cut a piece of fiberglass screen to fit inside the conch shell. It doesn't have to be perfect since this layer will be hidden. Pour a layer of horticultural charcoal over the screen to keep the terrarium tidy and fresh.

3. Create a substrate layer. Pour a generous amount of succulent soil mix into the conch shell. Leave about 1 in. (2.5 cm) between the top of the soil and the top of the vessel. This will allow enough room for the plants and topdressing elements to sit on top of the soil without spilling over. You can use a bamboo skewer to make shallow wells in the soil where your plants will be planted. At this point, I also like to experiment with plant placement. This beautiful cascading string of pearls looks like it was made for this particular spot, spilling out in dramatic fashion and adding a dynamic element to our scene.

4. Add the plants. Gently remove plants from pots and place in the prepared wells you created in the soil. Completely cover the roots with soil and firmly pat down the soil around the plants. Once the terrarium is complete, place a *Tillandsia bulbosa* Belize between the aloe and *Senecio rowleyanus*. Air plants love the humidity found in bathrooms, so I often rotate air plants through this terrarium to give them a little extra humidity before returning them to their home on a bookshelf!

5. Add topdressing. Pour white sand over the soil and use a flattening tool to spread the sand between each plant until the soil is completely covered.

6. Add decorative elements. As the tide recedes we find exposed coral, shells, and beach sand. For the tide, use crushed glass in turquoise. Pour the glass along the front side of the planter. Next, add a selenite crystal and three seashells along the waterfront, and then sprinkle crushed shells over the beach sand.

TERRARIUM CARE

Water once week with ½ cup (120 mL) of water. Remove the air plant and soak in water for 20 minutes once a week; allow to dry completely before adding back to display. Provide plenty of bright, indirect light.

CACTUSVILLE

SPIRIT OF THE SOUTHWEST

The cactus is clearly having its moment in the sun—literally! The millennial cactus craze has catapulted this humble, spiny plant into an overnight sensation. From bedsheets to wallpaper, cactus motifs are everywhere. And while I'm never one to turn my back on a trend, the cactus is quintessentially a symbol of the American Southwest. If the Southwest calls to your spirit, then you'll appreciate this "canyonland"-inspired terrarium. Place it in a bright room with plenty of sunlight and watch your own personal national park grow!

VESSEL
- 10 in. (25 cm) fishbowl

FOUNDATION
- 1½ cups (350 mL) aquarium gravel (brown)
- 2 cups (475 mL) orange sand
- ½ cup (120 mL) horticultural charcoal
- 1 lb. (½ kg) burnt orange sand (fine)
- fiberglass screen sheet

PLANTS
- 1 x *Haworthia fasciata*
- 1 x *Gymnocalycium mihanovichii* Moon Cactus
- 1 x *Mammillaria hahniana* Old Lady Cactus
- 1 x *Euphorbia mammillaris* Indian Corn Cob
- 1 x *Rebutia krainziana*
- 1 x *Mammillaria gracilis fragilis* Thimble Cactus

DECORATIVE ELEMENTS
- 1 x raw lepidolite stone
- 5 x rocks (raw agate, red stone, and river rocks)
- 1 x small piece of driftwood

TOOLS AND MATERIALS
- scissors
- 1 x magazine or newspaper sheet (folded)

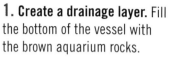

1. Create a drainage layer. Fill the bottom of the vessel with the brown aquarium rocks.

2. Add a separation layer. To prevent sand and soil from falling into the drainage layer, cut a piece of fiberglass screen and place it over the aquarium gravel.

3. Create a filtration layer.
This layer will be hidden, so only add charcoal in the center and over the fiberglass screen.

4. Add a decorative sand layer.
Pour orange sand all along the inside of the vessel. This will help hide the charcoal and soil layer. To create a more interesting landscape, layer the back and right side of the vessel with more sand than in the front.

5. Arrange cacti without getting pricked. If you don't have puncture-resistant gardening gloves to protect your skin from cactus spines, not to worry! Rip out a page from a magazine or newspaper, fold it over in 1 in. (2.5 cm) increments several times, and then fold it in half around the base the cactus. Pinch the paper together to lift the cactus out of its pot and position it inside the terrarium. Arrange smaller succulents in the front of the terrarium first and work your way toward the back with the tallest ones.

6. Add sand landscaping. Use scissors to snip off a corner of the sand bag (burnt orange). If your sand did not come in a small bag, either use a funnel or transfer it into a small freezer bag. Slowly pour sand along the inside edge of the vessel and between plants. Add more sand in some areas and less in others for a more dynamic look.

TERRARIUM CARE

This terrarium practically takes care of itself as long as you can provide bright light all day; placing it near a south-facing window is best. Provide ½ cup (120 mL) of water every 10 to 14 days during the warmer months and less in the winter.

7. Add decorative elements. Take brown aquarium gravel (the same used for the drainage layer) and sprinkle it around those plants in the center of the terrarium. When you water your succulents, the gravel will keep the water from running toward the front of the terrarium. Next, add the large agate rock in the center and smaller stones throughout. Firmly press the rocks into the sand. If you have a piece of driftwood, add it vertically next to the *Gymnocalycium mihanovichii* in the back.

DARLING DINO

A TERRARIUM OF PREHISTORIC PROPORTIONS

If you've ever made the drive from Los Angeles to Palm Springs, you've probably seen a pair of hundred-ton dinosaurs peeking through the trees! These larger-than-life dinosaur sculptures are so photogenic that they have their own social media account. But before they were stars, the Cabazon dinosaurs were just a regular stop on our annual family road trip. My dad was notorious for never stopping at the same place twice, but with my little brother and I repeatedly chanting "dinos, dinos, dinos" from the backseat, he really had no choice!

In this scene, a sparkly brontosaurus (as you can tell, I glammed her up a bit) meanders through a garden of unique succulents in search of her favorite snack. I love how this terrarium tells the story from any angle. Display as a centerpiece or on a coffee table, and your friends are sure to *raawr* over your new statement piece.

VESSEL
- 10 in. (25 cm) round glass bowl

FOUNDATION
- 12 x black river pebbles
- fiberglass screen sheet (or sphagnum moss)
- 5 cups (1.2 L) black aquarium sand
- ½ cup (120 mL) horticultural charcoal
- 3 cups (700 mL) succulent soil mix

PLANTS
- 1 x *Faucaria tigrina* Tiger Jaws
- 1 x *Haworthia retusa* Star Cactus
- 1 x *Gasteria bicolor* v. *liliputana* Dwarf Gasteria
- 1 x *Crassula marginalis rubra*
- 1 x *Echeveria* 'Deranosa'
- 1 x *Haworthia attenuata* Zebra Plant
- 1 x *Crassula mesembryanthemoides*

DECORATIVE ELEMENTS
- 1 x plastic toy dinosaur (brontosaurus)
- 1 x raw tourmaline stone

TOOLS AND MATERIALS
- drop cloth or newspaper
- scissors
- spoon (optional)
- metallic silver spray paint

BEFORE YOU BEGIN

Wash the plastic dinosaur in warm, soapy water and dry completely. The spray paint will stick to the plastic dinosaur better if the dinosaur is clean. In a well-ventilated area, cover your work surface with a drop cloth or newspaper to protect it from paint. Make sure your plants are a safe distance away from any paint fumes, as they could be harmful.

1. Spray paint the dinosaur.

Place the dinosaur on the drop cloth. Hold the paint can about 12 in. (30.5 cm) from the dinosaur and spray light, even coats to avoid drips. Allow paint to dry per product instructions (about 20 minutes). Add two or three coats until you achieve a bright metallic color. Once dry, run the dinosaur under water to remove any fume residue that may be harmful to your plants. Set it aside to dry while you get started on the terrarium.

2. Add a drainage layer.

Place the glass bowl on an even surface and add black river pebbles to the bottom of the bowl.

3. Add a filtration layer. Use scissors to cut a piece of fiberglass screen that fits into the bottom of the bowl. You can eyeball it—it doesn't have to be perfect because it will be completely hidden by the sand. Position the screen over the river pebbles. Next, sprinkle horticultural charcoal over the screen.

4. Create a substrate layer. Pour black aquarium sand into the bowl until the stones and screen are no longer visible. Next, add succulent soil to the center of the bowl. Fill to about 2 in. (5 cm) deep. I like to use a spoon so the dirt doesn't scatter everywhere. For a clean look, leave about 1 in. (2.5 cm) of sand around the inside perimeter of the bowl (we don't want the soil to show through the bowl).

PRO TIP!

What's great about going on vacation is that you usually come back with a few unshakeable vacation memories. How can you translate them into modern terrarium designs? A Hawaiian vacation, for instance? Easy: use tropical plants such as *Chamaedora elegans* 'Parlor Palm' and *Hypoestes* 'Triple Splash'. If a desert oasis is more your style, check out my Palm Springs-inspired terrarium on page 108. Once you have your terrarium done you'll be able to look at it and relive those memories!

5. Add succulents. Remove each succulent from its individual container and use your hands to massage away any excess potting soil. Plant your smallest succulents in the terrarium first. This will give you more room to maneuver before adding the largest plant. (Clockwise from the left: *Crassula marginalis rubra*, *Gasteria bicolor* v. *liliputana*, *Haworthia attenuata* Zebra Plant, *Faucaria tigrina*, *Haworthia retusa*, *Echeveria* 'Deranosa'.) As for the crassula, it will cascade beautifully over the bowl as it grows.

6. Add topdressing. The tallest succulent (*Crassula mesembryanthemoides*) is last to join the party. Completely cover the soil and base of succulents with black aquarium sand.

TERRARIUM CARE

Plants will begin to lean toward the nearest light source if left in one place too long. Give your terrarium a quarter turn every week to keep the plants straight and tall.

7. Add decorative elements. Finally, add a decorative tourmaline stone and place your dinosaur in the scene. From the front view, you'll have a beautiful minimalist look, and from the back, a lovely prehistoric garden.

DETOUR

Check out **#cabazondinosaurs** on Instagram.

DESERT OASIS

LET'S FLAMINGLE BY THE POOL

Palm Springs checks all the boxes for my ideal weekend getaway. Elvis honeymooned there—check! A wonderland of mid-century architecture—check! A botanical garden run by a cowboy and thousands of succulents to see—double check! Whether it's exploring the desert landscape or lounging by the pool, I'll never get tired of it. If I'm not in Palm Springs, then I'm probably daydreaming about Palm Springs.

For this terrarium project, we'll recreate a scene from my favorite vacation spot, complete with a retro Palm Springs-style home, frolicking lawn flamingos, and a sparkling pool! Along with other small succulents, these sweet mini cinnamon cacti are the perfect complement to our desert oasis. To top it all off, we'll create a layer of sand art that really makes this terrarium pop.

VESSEL
- 12 in. (30.5 cm) round glass bowl

FOUNDATION
- 4 cups (950 mL) aquarium gravel
- 2 cups (475 mL) succulent soil mix
- ¼ cup (60 mL) horticultural charcoal
- fiberglass screen sheet

PLANTS
- 2 x *Opuntia rufida minima* Cinnamon Cactus
- 3 x *Sedum rubrotinctum* 'Aurora' Pink Jelly Bean
- 1 x *Notocactus uebelmannianus*
- 2 x *Sempervivum jovibarba allionii*
- 2 x *Graptosedum* 'Darley Sunshine'
- 2 x *Pachyveria* 'Clavifolia' Jeweled Crown

DECORATIVE ELEMENTS
- ¼ cup (60 mL) blue sand
- 4 cups (950 mL) white sand
- 2 cups (475 mL) brown sand
- 4 cups (950 mL) brown aquarium gravel
- miniatures (for more information, visit www.acharmingproject.com/shop)
- 2 x miniature flamingos

TOOLS AND MATERIALS
- gloves
- long tweezers or newspaper (for handling cacti)
- spoon
- flattening tool (bamboo skewer and cork)

1. Add gravel. Fill the bottom of the vessel with brown aquarium gravel up to ½ in. (13 mm) deep. Give the bowl a good shake to evenly distribute the gravel and create a flat surface for your next foundation layer.

3. Add a retaining wall. Add gravel around the perimeter wall of the vessel—no more than 1 in. (2.5 cm) wide will do. This will contain the filtration layer and soil.

2. Create modern sand art. Start with a layer of white sand: pour a thin layer over the aquarium gravel. When working with layers of sand, I always suggest tapping the flattening tool over each layer to create even layers. Once the white sand is evenly distributed, pour in a thin layer of brown sand. Next, we'll create a repeating pattern all around the bowl. Press the end of the bamboo skewer against the glass and push the brown sand into the white sand. Repeat this step all around the vessel, leaving about ½ in. (13 mm) between each decorative line. Sandwich your decorative sand layer by pouring in another thin layer of white sand.

4. Add a filtration layer. Cut a fiberglass screen sheet in the shape of a circle to fit inside the retaining wall. It doesn't have to be a perfect circle, and you can approximate the measurements. The main purpose of this layer is to prevent the charcoal and soil from mixing with the sand.

5. Add horticultural charcoal. Cover the fiberglass screen with a thin layer of horticultural charcoal. I suggest using a spoon to protect your hands from the soot.

6. Add succulent mix. Fill the center of the vessel with succulent mix but avoid getting soil on the gravel. Use a skewer to create pockets for your succulents. It's always a good idea to preplan how to arrange succulents before planting them in the soil.

7. Plant the succulents. Remove the succulents and cacti from their pots. Before planting, clean off any excess soil from their roots. For the prickly cacti, use tweezers and a skewer to position them into place. If you don't have tweezers or tongs, you can hold cacti with newspaper and move them into place.

8. Add topdressing. Pour the white sand into the terrarium and spread it around the succulents until all of the soil is covered. I like using a skewer to get into all of the nooks and crannies.

9. Add decorative elements. Place the miniature Palm Springs home in front of your tall succulents. Press down until it sits snugly in place. Place two Sempervivum jovibarba allionii in front of the house, on either side of the door. The "pool" is simply a plastic outline shaped like a pool. Place the outline on top of the white sand and fill the inside with blue sand. Add a little blue sand at a time and use a bamboo skewer to spread evenly. Finally, add the miniature flamingos to the scene.

WATERING

Since you won't be able to see the soil to tell when it looks dry, it's important to keep to a watering schedule. For a vessel this size, 8 oz. (240 mL) of water every 1 to 2 weeks in the warm summer months should suffice. In the winter, succulents will become dormant and need only half the amount of water every 3 to 4 weeks.

LIGHT

These succulents and cacti require direct sunlight for at least 4 hours per day; placing them near a south- or east-facing window is recommended. If the stems of the succulents begin to elongate, they're letting you know they are not getting enough direct sunlight.

WHERE TO GET THE GOODS

If you would like to know more about this set, visit *www.acharmingproject.com/shop*.

A PLANT LOVER'S DREAM

PLANT YOUR OWN LIVING DREAM CATCHER AND WATCH IT GROW

In some Native American cultures, the dream catcher is viewed as a symbol of protection, hope, and healing. Originally, dream catchers were made from wooden hoops, and plant fibers were woven together to make the center web. It is believed that good dreams pass through the center opening, while nightmares are caught in the web until morning when they are destroyed by sunlight. How epic is that!? I can't help but want one in every room. In this project, we'll use air plants, succulents, and cascading Spanish moss to bring your dream catcher to life—literally!

VESSEL
- 8 in. (20 cm) grapevine wreath

PLANTS
- preserved Spanish moss in white
- 3 x *Echeveria* 'Blue Fairy'
- 3 x *Tillandsia usneoides* Spanish moss
- 1 x *Tillandsia stricta* (fine leaf)
- 1 x *Tillandsia harrisii*

TOOLS AND MATERIALS
- 6 ft. (2 m) cotton beading cord
- hot glue gun and glue sticks (floral glue works, too)
- 3 x twist ties
- scissors

1. Loop cord all the way around the vine. Take one end of the cotton cord and tie a knot to the top of the wreath. Make sure the knot is tight enough that it won't slide. Pull the cord about 2 in. (5 cm) from your starting point, and wrap the cord over the wreath, around, and through the open loop. Keep the cord taut at all times, but not tight enough to warp the wreath. Continue wrapping all the way around the wreath until you are back at the starting point.

2. Continue looping cord. Wrap the cord (over, around, and through) the midpoint of each section you previously completed. Continue wrapping this way until you only have a small opening in the center of the web.

3. Tie off and cut excess cord. When the web is complete, tie a knot to the midpoint of the final section and cut off the remaining cord.

4. Attach live Spanish moss. Gather one bunch of Spanish moss and attach it to the bottom of the wreath with a twist tie. Attach a total of three bunches. You may need more depending on how large your nursery sells each bunch.

Not all glues are created equal. Using a hot glue gun is my favorite method because it gets the job done quickly. However, it's not water resistant. If you live in a humid climate, you may want to use floral glue instead. I do recommend using a low-temperature glue gun to avoid damaging plant leaves. When gluing stems, it's important not to drench them with glue. Leave a little breathing room, so new roots can grow.

5. Hot glue the preserved moss. Hot glue several clumps of preserved Spanish moss to the bottom half of the wreath. This will hide the twist ties and give the succulents something to root into.

6. Prepare succulent cuttings. Use sharp scissors to cut the stems of each echeveria just below the leaves. Leave about ¼ in. (6 mm) of the stem intact. This will allow the stem to continue to produce roots.

7. Glue succulents to the display. Decide how you would like to arrange your echeveria. Apply a generous amount of glue to the stems of each succulent (be careful not to scorch the leaves) and press them firmly into the preserved Spanish moss. Hold them in place until the glue begins to set.

8. Add air plants. Next, position air plants on both sides of the dream catcher and glue their bases to the wreath. Hold them in place until completely dry.

TERRARIUM CARE

A display like this can last a few months, depending on the health of your plants at time of purchase and amount of light the display receives. After a couple of months, the succulents will sprout roots and will need to be removed and repotted. You can always add new succulents to the dream catcher as time goes on.

Hang your dream catcher in a place with bright indirect sunlight. Mist Spanish moss frequently to keep it green and healthy (every couple of days). In colder months, you may only need to mist once or twice a week. Keep in mind that it is natural for your succulents to shed a few leaves nearest to the stems, and it's no cause for alarm. However, if the leaves start to brown, or leaves fall from the center, it's time to remove the succulents. Simply pluck them from the display, clean off the glue, and repot them.

A MOSSY OCCASION

I MOSS FIND MY SEAT

Planning a special occasion? Help your guests find their names and take their seats! Whether you're inviting a few friends over for brunch or throwing a big celebratory affair, you can impress your guests with their very own mossarium party favors!

Reindeer moss comes in a variety of colors to fit any color scheme or theme, and, once the party is over, guests can take home their mossarium party favors and display them anywhere they like. Best of all, this moss is preserved and requires no maintenance whatsoever. Party on, moss!

VESSEL
- 6 oz. (175 mL) mini round glass bottle with cork

FOUNDATION
- silver decorative rocks

PLANTS
- preserved reindeer moss in mint green, purple, and orange

DECORATIVE ELEMENTS
- 2 in. (5 cm) wire eye pins
- place cards
- double-sided tape
- gold alphabet stickers

TOOLS AND MATERIALS
- bamboo skewer
- funnel

1. Add a layer of decorative rocks. Use a funnel to pour silver rocks into your bottle. Fill the vessel until it is about one-fourth full. Another option would be to fill the bottle with sand or seashells.

2. Add moss. Use a bamboo skewer to push moss into the bottle. Pack it in tightly before adding each new layer. I used three different colors of moss, but you can use as few or as many as you please.

3. Add guest names to place cards. My handwriting is okay, but it's not perfect, which is why I love using alphabet stickers for this step. Stickers are quick and easy, and you don't need to worry about ink smudges. Plus, if you accidently misspell a friend's name, you can just pop off a letter and replace it with the correct one!

BRIGHT IDEA!

For large parties, you can add a sticker indicating the table number directly on the front of the bottle and use these as escort cards to help your friends and family find their tables.

4. Top off the cork with the place card. If you dabble in jewelry making, then you are probably familiar with eye pins and possibly even make your own using metal wire and roundnose pliers. You can also buy them from your local craft store, as I did. Place one eye pin inside the place card and adhere with double-sided tape. Close the card and press down firmly to secure in place. Insert the eye pin into the top of your cork. Pop the cork into the bottle and place your mossarium bottles to help guide your guests to their seats.

FERN FEVER

SAY HELLO TO MY LITTLE FRONDS

Let me start by saying that, if it were not for the invention of terrariums, I could not keep a single fern in our apartment. Ferns need the perfect balance of high humidity, water, and shade to live long, happy lives. One whiff of the bone-dry air in my place would surely spell doom for these tropical prima donnas. If you have the same dilemma as me, keeping ferns inside a closed terrarium guarantees you've won half the battle!

Nothing makes me happier than to provide a happy home for ferns. In this project, we will enclose ferns in a beautifully crafted glass house, where their ornate leaves can be admired from all sides. Smooth river pebbles add a striking contrast to the glass and metal structure, while bright clumps of pincushion moss make distinguished companions for our ferns.

VESSEL
- 8¼ in. (21 cm) square x 8¼ in. (21 cm) high antique zinc glass house (available from World Market)

FOUNDATION
- 4 cups (950 mL) mix of river pebbles
- fiberglass screen sheet
- 2 cups (475 mL) potting soil mix
- ¼ cup (60 mL) horticultural charcoal

PLANTS
- 8 x *Leucobryum glaucum* Pincushion Moss
- 1 x *Nephrolepis cordifolia* 'Duffii' Lemon Button Fern
- 1 x *Polystichum tsus-simense* Korean Rock Fern
- 1 x *Hemionitis arifolia* Heart Fern

TOOLS AND MATERIALS
- gloves
- scissors
- spoon (optional)
- ruler (optional)

1. Add river pebbles. Evenly spread river pebbles over the floor of the glass house. Fill to about 1 in. (2.5 cm) deep.

2. Create a filtration layer. Cut the fiberglass screen sheet in the shape of a square to fit inside the vessel. You can eyeball the measurements, or you can use a ruler to precisely measure and cut to size. Lay the screen over the river pebbles.

3. Sprinkle in charcoal. Layer a thin layer of horticultural charcoal over the fiberglass screen. Use a spoon or garden gloves to protect your hands from soot.

4. Add more river pebbles and the soil layer. Create a retaining wall by adding river pebbles around the inside perimeter of the vessel. This will help keep the fiberglass from rolling up and will hide the soil. Spread potting soil in the center of the container and fill to 1 in. (2.5 cm) deep.

5. Remove ferns from pots and place inside. Removing ferns from pots can be a messy and delicate procedure. If you have a pair of gardening gloves, this would be a good time to use them. Carefully turn each pot on its side and tap the sides and bottom of the pot to loosen the soil. Once the ferns are free from their pots, clean off the excess soil and dead leaves. Arrange all three ferns close to the center of the container so that their leaves are not pressed up against the glass. I like to add the two smaller ones in the back and the largest one in last. Generously cover the root balls with additional potting mix.

6. Decorate. For an extra touch of green, surround the ferns with clumps of moss. Pincushion moss does very well in a closed container, and you'll notice it starting to turn a vibrant green after it soaks in the humidity for a day. Cover any visible potting mix with river pebbles.

TERRARIUM CARE

As the ferns grown you will need to occasionally prune the fronds back away from the glass. However, letting them grow a little wild can be extremely appealing, too! If you notice any fronds turning brown it means the soil is too dry. Give them a drink and trim away any brown bits. Be on the lookout for too much condensation on the inside of the glass. If water droplets begin to form on the glass, crack open the lid for a few hours to allow excess moisture to escape. Ferns and moss love shady environments. Keep away from direct sunlight.

7. Add water. Before closing the lid of the glass house, mist the moss and as close to the fern roots as you can get. Avoid watering directly on the leaves to prevent water rot. Misting will not only water the plants but also give them an added kick of humidity. Alternatively, you can add 2 oz. (60 mL) of water using a squeeze bottle. Since these types of containers are rarely airtight, the moisture will escape, so you may need to add water weekly.

GO WITH THE FAUX

SOMETIMES YOU GOTTA FAKE IT TILL YOU MAKE IT

For us apartment dwellers, terrariums provide the perfect ecosystems to help our plants survive indoors. Even so, I can name three spots in my apartment that are total "kill zones" (complete with caution tape and chalk outlines of foliage!). I've tried keeping succulents, flowers, and houseplants in those areas, and, for one reason or another, they never survive. If you have an area of your home with a survival rate of zero, allow me to introduce you to the joy of being an artificial plant owner. This faux succulent display is one of my favorite no-maintenance displays. It's a perfect addition to any dorm room, office, or dark place in your home that needs a little color.

VESSEL
- 13 x 13 x 1½ in. (33 x 33 x 3.8 cm) tray

FOUNDATION
- floral foam (cut to fit the size of your tray)

PLANTS
- 40 x artificial succulents

DECORATIVE ELEMENTS
- reindeer moss

TOOLS AND MATERIALS
- serrated knife

1. Cut floral foam to fit your tray. Floral foam comes in all shapes and sizes. Be sure to buy the exact size of your tray or a little bigger and use a serrated knife to cut it to size. It should fit snugly inside the tray. If you find you have some space between the foam and wall of the tray, not to worry—you can fill this in with moss later.

2. Add succulents. Insert the stem of each succulent into the floral foam. I suggest starting from the center and working your way out to the edges of the tray. Leave some room between succulents where you will add moss.

3. Add reindeer moss. Use a hot glue gun to glue pieces of colored moss between your succulents. If you have any gaps around the tray, fill them in with moss. This tray has cutout handles on two of its sides, so I glued moss inside the cutouts to hide the floral moss. Lay on a flat surface or stand upright in a bookcase or on a desk.

GREEN LANTERN

THE FUNGI AMONG US

Say good-bye to those tacky nightlight plug-ins! Usher in a more peaceful and natural bedside companion with this minimalist glow-in-the-dark terrarium. By day, this Scandinavia-inspired lantern adds a touch of natural décor to your bedroom or kid's room. By night, fall asleep to the soft glow of your own handmade nightlight. Using glow-in-the-dark clay and a couple of tools, it's easy to sculpt your fungi forest inhabitants.

While they may look like mosses, fruticose lichen are actually fungi! They make the perfect ground cover for our modern forest scene. Lichen is easy to maintain and requires only weekly misting. Forgot to mist your lichen? Not a biggie. Just soak it in water for a few minutes, and it will come back to life before your very eyes!

VESSEL
- 11½ in. high x 7¾ in. diameter (29 cm high x 20 cm diameter) UTSTRÅLNING lantern in black (from Ikea)

FOUNDATION
- 2 cups (475 mL) peat moss
- ⅔ cup (160 mL) horticultural charcoal
- 4 cups (950 mL) blue river rocks

PLANTS
- 8 x fruticose lichen mounds

DECORATIVE ELEMENTS
- 2 oz. (57 g) Sculpey III Oven-Bake Clay (Glow in the Dark)

TOOLS AND MATERIALS
- paintbrush (or any tool with a handle that has a rounded top)
- 4 x 2 in. (5 cm) jewelry eye pins (or floral wire)

BEFORE YOU BEGIN

Wash the river rocks with warm, soapy water and allow to air dry.

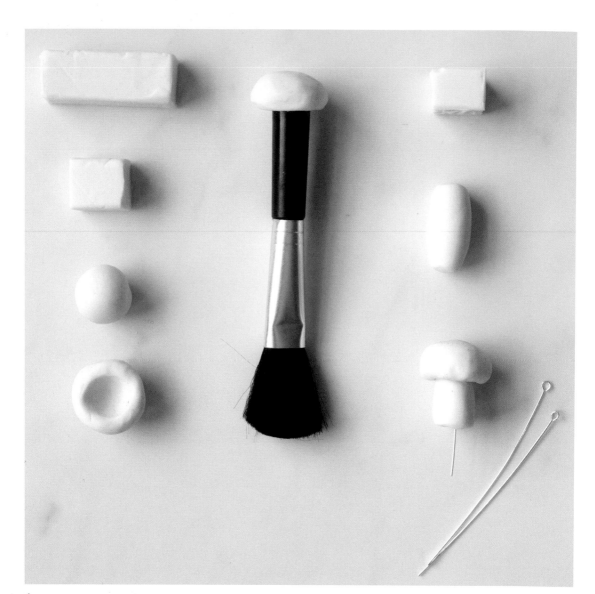

1. Mold mushrooms out of clay. Sculpey polymer clay is available online and at most craft stores and comes with four bars to a pack. To make the mushroom cap, break off a piece that is one-third the size of one brick. Roll the clay between the palms of your hands until you have a ball. Place the ball over the top handle of a paintbrush and use your fingers to mold the clay to look like a mushroom cap. Gently remove the clay from the handle and set aside. To make the stem, cut another one-third piece of clay and roll forward and backward between the palms of your hands until you have what looks like a mushroom stem. Use your fingers to flatten the top and bottom of the stem. Add the mushroom cap to the stem. To secure the mushroom cap to the stem and give us a way to anchor the mushroom to the lichen use a jewelry eye pin or floral wire. Press the eye pin into the stem until you reach the mushroom cap. Repeat these steps to make a total of four mushrooms. Place your clay mushrooms on a nonstick pan and bake in the oven according to instructions on the label. The average is about 15 minutes at 275°F (130°C).

2. Create the drainage layer. Generally, this layer serves as our water reservoir. However, there is no need to drench lichen with water, which means this will be more of a decorative layer. Fill with any type of rocks or decorative pebbles you wish (I love the look of blue river pebbles). Gently pour river pebbles into the lantern and then pick up the lantern and give it a good shake to create an even layer.

3. Create a filtration layer. Add in your horticultural charcoal so that it just covers the river pebbles. Since we will not be drenching the soil with water, the charcoal will simply serve to keep the foundation layer fresh and fight off any chance of mold.

4. Add the foundation layer. As with moss, I like to use a slightly acidic soil with my lichen, but potting soil will do just fine. Fill with peat moss soil mix to about 1 in. (2.5 cm) in height.

5. Arrange lichen inside vessel. Lichen generally comes in small mounds. Place the mounds over soil and arrange them so that there is no space left between them. Firmly press down on the lichen to avoid any air pockets, which could lead to unwanted bacteria.

6. Arrange mushrooms. Place your clay mushrooms in the scene by pressing the wires and stems down into the forest floor. Add all four mushrooms (or as many or as little as you like.)

RECHARGE!

Naturally recharge your nightlight by removing the top and holding the terrarium under a light source for a few minutes.

MOSSY PICCHU

ALPACA MY BAGS FOR PERU

Creating a miniature garden that mimics our own natural world is one of the most addictive aspects of terrarium making. There are so many locations and environments to draw inspiration from that it can be overwhelming. If you're feeling stuck, and searching for a theme, consider basing your terrarium design around a miniature figurine.

In this scene, we find an alpaca looking out over the mountainous Andean highlands that it calls home. Pincushion moss and mood moss help create the look of grass and shrubs. Meanwhile, river pebbles cascade downward, giving the appearance of height. The multiple layers below the moss are just as beautiful and complement the entire highland scene.

VESSEL
- 6 x 11 in. (15 x 28 cm) apothecary jar with lid

FOUNDATION
- 3 cups (700 mL) beige aquarium gravel
- 1½ cups (350 mL) black sand
- 2 cups (475 mL) sphagnum moss
- 1 cup (240 mL) horticultural charcoal
- 4 cups (950 mL) peat moss soil mix

PLANTS
- *Dicranum scoparium* Mood Moss
- 5 x mounds *Leucobryum glaucum* Pincushion Moss

DECORATIVE ELEMENTS
- 1 x alpaca figurine (for more information, visit *www.acharmingproject.com/shop*)
- 1 cup (240 mL) river pebbles

TOOLS AND MATERIALS
- E6000 glue

1. Create a foundation layer. Add beige aquarium rocks to the to the bottom of the vessel.

2. Add a decorative base layer. Pour a layer of black sand over the gravel. Alternating between light and dark layers really makes the scene pop.

3. Add a filtration layer.
Because this is a closed terrarium, condensation will appear on the inside of the vessel and run down the sides into the foundation layer. Sphagnum moss will help with filtration.

4. Add charcoal. This layer will help with filtration and help control the growth of mold.

5. Set the foundation for your landscape. Start by pouring peat moss inside the terrarium. Here is where you get to determine the height and shape of the landscape. To create height, tilt the vessel in the direction you would like to look higher and use your hands to spread the peat moss in that direction. Mold the landscape to your liking. If this seems difficult because your soil is too dry, give it a very light mist of water so that it's easier to work with.

6. Add greenery. Press moss mounds firmly into the soil. Do not leave any air pockets between the soil and moss (this could lead to mold or fungus growth). Next take bits of mood moss and place all around the inside of the terrarium nearest to the glass. Its unruly nature means it won't mind if it gets pushed up against the glass a bit. Leave an opening between the moss mounds for the rocky bits.

TERRARIUM CARE

Allow moss to acclimate to its new environment for 24 hours before watering. Mosses absorb water through their foliage, so directly misting the leaves is the best way to go. Set the mossarium in a place where it will receive indirect sunlight or in an office environment under fluorescent lamps. If the lid is not airtight, you will occasionally need to mist the moss to introduce moisture. If too much condensation appears on the inside of the vessel, leave the lid open for a few hours to allow excess moisture to escape. Mold may appear in the form of gray filaments. This could just be the moss acclimating to its new environment, or it could be a sign of too much moisture. Use a cotton swab to remove the mold and leave the terrarium open until the mold disappears.

7. Add rocky bits and the figurine. Fill the space between the mosses with river pebbles so they look like they are cascading down a mountain. As for the alpaca, add a few dots of glue to the underside of its feet to attach it to a river pebble. Allow it to dry, about 20 minutes, before adding it to the terrarium. Finish by placing the lid on your new terrarium.

WILL YOU MARI-MO ME?

TWO HEARTS BEAT BETTER THAN ONE

These lovable balls of furry algae are easily the cutest and most unique plants you'll ever have the pleasure of owning. Native to Japan, *Cladophora aegagropila linnaei* is affectionately called *marimo,* which literally translates to "ball of algae." Legend has it that centuries ago in Japan, a lord's daughter fell in love with a commoner. Their love was forbidden, and they were forced to flee so they could be together. Soon after, marimo balls miraculously appeared in Lake Akan—a fact attributed to the power of the couple's unbreakable love. Ever since, marimo balls have been regarded as a symbol of love and are often given as gifts. For this reason, I can't help but always display marimo balls in pairs. Don't they look cozy together?

VESSEL
- 10 x 10 in. (25 x 25 cm) flat-sided glass vase or fishbowl

FOUNDATION
- 2 cups (475 mL) white sand
- 1 cup (240 mL) white river pebbles
- filtered water

PLANTS
- 2 x *Cladophora aegagropila linnaei* (marimo balls)

DECORATIVE ELEMENTS
- 9 in. (23 cm) dried coral sea fan

TOOLS AND MATERIALS
- chopsticks
- funnel
- spoon (optional)
- squeeze bottle with narrow nozzle

BEFORE YOU BEGIN

Whether you purchase your sea fan online or in person at your local aquarium store, it's a good idea to give it a quick rinse. Same goes for the *Cladophora aegagropila linnaei* (marimo balls): give them a quick rinse under water and then a good squeeze before placing them inside the vessel.

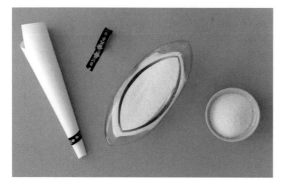

1. Add a layer of sand. The opening of the container is narrow, so it's best to use a funnel to add the foundation layer of sand. If you don't already have a plastic funnel, it's super easy to make your own. Roll up an ordinary sheet of copy paper and secure it with a piece of tape. Then use the funnel to add white sand to the bottom of the vessel, 1 in. (2.5 cm) deep. To keep the sand from clouding the glass, keep the end of the funnel close to the bottom of the vessel.

2. Place the sea fan inside the container. Gently push the sea fan down into the sand until it touches the bottom of the vessel. You have the option of cutting the sea fan with scissors to fit inside the container, but I prefer to leave it intact.

3. Add a rocky layer. Cover the sand with rocks so when we pour the water into the vessel, the sand doesn't mix with the water and appear murky. Add white pebbles to a depth of 2 in. (5 cm) in front and behind the sea fan to help hold it in place. Be careful not to damage the sea fan when adding in the pebbles. Optional: use a long spoon to lower pebbles down into the vessel.

4. Add marimo balls. Use chopsticks to lower each marimo ball into the vessel and place them side by side.

5. Fill the vessel up with water. I like to use a squeeze bottle with a narrow nozzle to pour water down the inside of the vessel so as not to kick up the sand and muddy the water.

TERRARIUM CARE

Marimos are native to the cold, dark waters of lakes. For this reason, keep marimos in low-light conditions and away from hot windows. If your marimos begin to turn brown, move them to a cooler, darker location. Keep marimos round and fluffy (nobody likes bed head) by occasionally rotating them and giving them a gentle squeeze. Add fresh water once every two weeks. If algae begin to grow on the inside of the vessel, wipe it away with a clean sponge and refill with fresh water.

SUCCULENT COCKTAIL

WITH FRESHLY CUT GARNISH

This project is easily one of my favorites because at first glance it looks like a fun, glitzy succulent garden. But don't be fooled! This shaken-not-stirred martini glass serves a greater purpose as a temporary home for new succulent cuttings. In the plant-enthusiast world, there is nothing more gratifying that propagating your own succulents (see page 235 to learn how you can do it). The idea of turning one plant into as many as twenty new plants not only brings personal satisfaction but also can be cost effective when the time comes to make a new terrarium! There is always the question of where to keep cuttings. This project is a beautiful way to keep your cuttings in a safe place until the stems sprout roots and you are ready to plant them in their new terrariums. Finally, no martini is complete without a couple of "olives" to garnish!

VESSEL
- 10 in. (25 cm) oversized novelty martini glass

FOUNDATION
- 18 oz. (530 mL) jar of pink glass gems and white marbles

PLANTS
- 1 x bag of naturally dried Spanish moss
- 1 x sheet of MossyMat Peel and Stick (preserved moss for craft projects)
- cuttings from various echeverias

DECORATIVE ELEMENTS
- 1 x bamboo skewer
- 2 x 1 in. (2.5 cm) Styrofoam balls

TOOLS AND MATERIALS
- scissors
- green spool of thread

DON'T HAVE SUCCULENT CUTTINGS QUITE YET?

Some online wholesalers and nurseries will sell you succulent cuttings for a fraction of the price of plants. Search online or ask around! You could also use air plants as a substitution for succulent cuttings.

1. Create a foundation layer. Pour in glass gems and marbles, leaving a space of about 2 in. (5 cm) from the top rim of the glass.

2. Add Spanish moss. Pile on pieces of Spanish moss over the decorative glass gems. Form a loose dome shape and avoid pressing down on the moss. Leaving the moss loose will leave room to add our succulent cuttings and give the roots room to grow.

3. Arrange the plants. Take your succulent cuttings and place the roots directly into the Spanish moss. Completely fill the container, leaving no space between succulents.

4. Create moss balls. Use scissors to roughly cut a 4 in. (10 cm) circle of MossyMat. Peel off the paper backing and place the Styrofoam ball in the center (on the side that is sticky). Next, fold the corners of the sheet moss inward until the ball is completely covered. The ball may look a little heavy on one side, but the next step will take care of that.

5. Wrap with thread. Your ball may look a little heavy on one side where you folded the sheet moss over itself. Not to worry! Take green thread and begin wrapping the thread all around the moss ball. Shape the ball into a circle by pulling tighter in areas that need to be flattened. When you feel you have formed a tight and well-shaped ball, tie off the thread with a double knot and cut the excess with scissors.

TERRARIUM CARE

Bright indirect light is the best way to keep this display from drying out too quickly. In perfect condition, this terrarium will last a month, with no watering necessary, before the plants need to be planted in soil and watered.

BRIGHT IDEA!

Invite all of your friends over for a terrarium party! Set out small glass fishbowls or mason jars on a table, along with basic terrarium tools, for each of your friends. In the center of the table, lay out different trays with rocks, charcoal, soil, and decorative elements, such as shells, gemstones, and reindeer moss. Lastly, set this fabulous succulent martini glass in the center of the table and have your friends pluck out their favorite cuttings and plant in their own mini terrariums.

6. Make the cocktail stirrer. Take the sharp end of a bamboo skewer and carefully push through the moss ball. Repeat this with the second moss ball, making sure to leave space between the two. Place the "olive pick" in one side of the martini glass. The marbles should hold it in position. This living martini glass can be used to decorate your at-home bar or be the centerpiece for a terrarium party!

GEO MINIMAL

SIMPLY PRICKLY

The zebra plant *(Haworthia attenuata)* is the lazy gardener's best friend. Architecturally beautiful to look at, this plant grows at a snail's pace and is incredibly tolerant of underwatering. In this project, I will show you how to make a quick terrarium by reusing the plastic pot your plant came in. It will be a long time before you will need to repot this plant, unless offsets begin shooting from the parent plant. In that case, repot once the offset is one-third the size of the parent plant, and then you will have two plants for the price of one!

This geometric terrarium with its sleek lines and aura of sophistication engages anyone with a modern or minimalist aesthetic. Amenable to low-light conditions more than other succulents, it's right at home on a coffee table, nightstand, or office desk. This simple haworthia terrarium is as easy as it gets.

VESSEL
- 4¾ x 4¾ x 9½ in. (12 x 12 x 24 cm) black triangle glass

FOUNDATION
- 1½ cup (350 mL) white sand
- 8 x small white pebbles

PLANTS
- *Haworthia attenuata* Zebra Plant

DECORATIVE ELEMENTS
- gypsum crystal (desert rose)

TOOLS AND MATERIALS
- scissors
- mini shovel or spoon
- tacky glue (optional)

BEFORE YOU BEGIN

Wash the river pebbles with warm, soapy water and allow to dry completely. If you find any gaps in in your geometric vessel where the sand will pour out, use tacky glue to close the gaps. Wait 30 minutes or until the glue is dry before adding your plant.

1. Prepare the vessel. If your vessel has any gaps where the sand may pour out, use tacky glue to cover the gaps. Wait around 30 minutes or until the glue is completely dry before adding your plant.

2. Prepare the plant pot. Most small plants come in 2 in. (5 cm) containers. You may need to cut the top of the container to fit your geometric vessel without having sand spill over the edge of the opening. Remove the plant from the container. Use scissors to cut and discard the top of the container—about ½ in. (13 mm).

3. Add a drainage layer. Line the bottom of the plant container with a few small pebbles. This will help prevent the plant roots from sitting in water too long after watering.

4. Repot the haworthia. Place the plant back in its original pot with the same soil mix it came in. You can also add fresh soil if you have some on hand. Use a mini shovel or spoon to cover the soil with sand.

5. Add the plant and decorative element. Arrange the haworthia inside the vessel so that it is centered. Fill the inside of the vessel with white sand until the only thing visible is the plant. Finally, place a gypsum crystal adjacent to the plant.

TERRARIUM CARE

Place in an area with bright indirect light. Though the haworthia may look like it can handle a lot of sunlight, direct sunlight will scorch its leaves. I suggest using a plastic syringe to water only the base of the plant. About 1 oz. (30 mL) of water every 10 to 12 days will do.

PRICKLY BY NATURE

LOOK BEYOND THE PRICKLY SURFACE TO FIND THE BEAUTY BENEATH!

Books and plants often compete for space on our shelves. Help them get along by making a functional space for both to dwell in. First, repurpose ordinary glass candleholders into mini terrarium pots for each of your succulents. Next, get in touch with your artistic side and create your own colorful sand art inside two unassuming magazine holders. These living bookends make for an unexpected twist on any bookshelf.

VESSEL
- 2 x acrylic magazine holders
- 6 x glass votive candleholders

FOUNDATION
- ¼ cup (60 mL) horticultural charcoal
- 1½ cups (350 mL) succulent soil
- 1 cup (240 mL) sphagnum moss

PLANTS
- 2 x *Haworthia reinwardtii*
- 1 x *Haworthia coarctata*
- 1 x *Haworthia attenuata* Zebra Plant
- 1 x *Haworthia attenuata* 'Enon'
- 2 x *Gymnocalycium mihanovichii* Moon Cactus

DECORATIVE ELEMENTS
- 7 cups (1.7 L) coarse white sand
- 4 cups (950 mL) coarse pink sand
- 4 cups (950 mL) coarse beige sand
- 2½ cups (590 mL) coarse black sand
- 1 cup (240 mL) small river rocks

TOOLS AND MATERIALS
- flattening tool (bamboo skewer and cork)
- sheet of paper
- piece of tape
- mini shovel or spoon
- small natural hairbrush
- plastic syringe for watering

1. Add foundation layers.
Fill half of the first votive glass with river rocks, sphagnum moss, and a pinch of horticultural charcoal. Fill the rest of the vessel with succulent soil mix. Repeat these steps for each votive glass.

2. Plant your succulents.
Place each succulent in its own votive glass and cover the roots with soil. Taller succulents will especially want to lean to one side if the soil is too loose. Firmly press down on the topsoil to secure in place.

3. Add a decorative base layer. Use a funnel to fill the vessel with ¼ in. (6 mm) of white sand. Use a flattening tool to pat down and level the sand. Next, place your first succulent (*Haworthia coarctata*) inside the container.

4. Add the next layer of sand. Add beige sand to the vessel using the funnel. To give the look of peaks and valleys, pour small piles of sand around the inside throughout the container.

5. Add the next layer of sand and succulents.
Pour a layer of white sand into the container
and snugly place two more succulents inside
the terrarium (*Haworthia reinwardtii* and
Gymnocalycium mihanovichii), leaving a little
room between them. Next, add a layer of black
sand, one of pink sand, and a final layer of
white sand until the votive glass pots are
completely covered.

6. Dust off each succulent using a small brush.
Take care to carefully remove any sand from
between leaves. To complete your set of bookends,
repeat the foregoing steps with a second acrylic
magazine holder.

TERRARIUM CARE

Place these terrariums near filtered sunlight. The best method for watering a sand art terrarium without disturbing the sandy design is to use a plastic syringe with a curved tip. Water directly at the base of each succulent every 12 to 14 days.

PRO TIP!

When working with sand, keep in mind that it can get everywhere, especially when pouring it into the terrarium. Using a funnel helps keep the sand contained and makes it easier to pour around the succulents and into tight corners. To prevent the inside of the terrarium from becoming "foggy" and requiring you to repeatedly wipe down the inside, keep the tip of the funnel pointed downward and just barely skim the surface as you pour the sand.

LITTLE MISS SUNSHINE

SOME LIKE IT HOT, HOT, HOT

My husband and I recently moved into what we consider our dream apartment. Hardwood floors, lots of windows, and plenty of space for all of my succulents and terrariums. All of this got me thinking . . . If succulents could design their own terrarium home, what would it be like? I imagine a Mid-Century Modern with a touch of sassy southwestern cactus wallpaper, sandy floors, and rocky accents throughout. It should go without saying that these desert divas love to bask in the sun, so their favorite pastime plays a big part in this sunny terrarium design. If you love crafting and love desert plants, then grab your glue gun, because it's about to get sunny up in here!

VESSEL
- 9 x 4 in. (23 x 10 cm) acrylic fish bubble wall mount

FOUNDATION
- 1½ cups (350 mL) lava rocks
- 1 cup (240 mL) sphagnum moss
- 1½ cups (350 mL) cactus soil mix
- ¼ cup (60 mL) horticultural charcoal
- ¾ cup (180 mL) beige sand

PLANTS
- 2 x *Mammillaria gracilis fragilis* Thimble Cactus
- 1 x *Chamaelobivia* 'Rose Quartz'
- 1 x *Sempervivum* 'Pacific Teddy'

DECORATIVE ELEMENTS
- 1 x jar yellow decorative glass rocks
- 2 x beach stones
- 1 x tiger eye
- small decorative rocks
- 12 x 12 in. (30.5 x 30.5 cm) gold foil card stock with cactus pattern

TOOLS AND MATERIALS
- pencil
- long tweezers
- small hand trowel or spoon
- scissors
- round hand punch
- funnel
- flattening tool (bamboo skewer and cork)
- nail
- hammer

1. Trace and cut the background for this scene. Lay the vessel down flat on the card stock. There is a small opening in the vessel from where you will hang it from a nail on the wall. Mark this spot on the card stock with your pencil. Use a pencil to trace all the way around the vessel. Use scissors to cut along the line until you have a perfect circle.

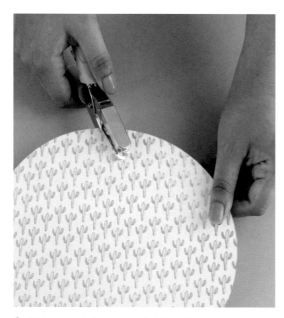

2. Hole punch for the nail. Find the spot you marked for the nail and use a hole punch to cut out a small circle.

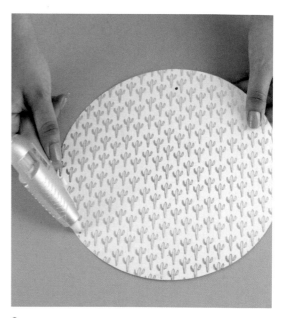

3. Add hot glue. Add a few dots of hot glue to the perimeter of the card stock, about 2 in. (5 cm) apart.

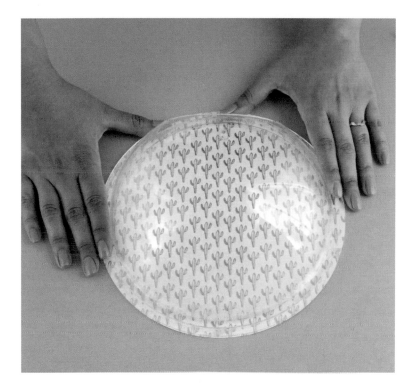

4. Glue the bubble to the background. Line up the flat side of the vessel with the card stock and press down the edges until the glue dries.

5. Add glass pebbles. Hot glue the perimeter of the vessel and press the flat side of the glass pebbles down into the glue. Hold down until fully dry (about 10 seconds). Be careful not to burn your fingers with hot glue.

6. Add the foundation layer. Use your hands or a spoon to pour lava rocks into the vessel, filling to about 2 in. (5 cm).

7. Create a filtration layer. For this project, we'll use sphagnum moss as the separation layer. Fill to about 1 in. (2.5 cm) deep. Long tweezers really help to fill in any gaps. Pour in the horticultural soil to keep the terrarium from getting too funky.

8. Add cactus soil. Pour cactus soil into the terrarium with your hand or paper funnel. Create a slope by adding less soil at the front than the back. Use the flattening tool to compact the soil and then use the bamboo skewer to make small pockets in the soil where you will plant your succulents and cacti.

9. Add plants. Carefully remove succulents and cacti from their pots using long tweezers and place them in the divots of soil you dug out for them. You may have to add additional cactus mix to make sure the roots are adequately covered.

10. Add topdressing. Cover the soil with beige sand using a paper funnel.

11. Add decorative elements. Use long tweezers to add pebbles around the inside of the terrarium. Cacti and hardy sempervivum succulents need 8 hours of sunlight per day. Hang the terrarium from a wall near a bright window or even outdoors on your balcony or patio.

SO JELLY

CATCH A GLIMPSE OF LIFE BENEATH THE SEA

In this seascape terrarium, you will combine a dried sea urchin and air plant to make a whimsical jellyfish. Here, beneath the tide, where the sunlight can still reach them, you'll use succulents bearing a remarkable resemblance to plants and corals most commonly found in shallow ocean waters. Scattered seashells complete this charming ocean-inspired scene—minus the salt water!

VESSEL
- 8½ x 16 in. (21.5 x 40.5 cm) glass apothecary vase

FOUNDATION
- 4 cups (950 mL) succulent soil mix
- 4 cups (950 mL) beige aquarium gravel
- ½ cup (120 mL) horticultural charcoal
- fiberglass screen sheet (or sphagnum moss)

PLANTS
- 2 x *Crassula ovata* 'Gollum' Jade Plant
- 1 x *Crassula ovata* 'Tricolor' Jade Plant
- 1 x *Adromischus cristatus* Crinkle Leaf Plant
- 1 x *Tillandsia stricta* (fine leaf)

DECORATIVE ELEMENTS
- 1 x purple and white sea urchin shell
- 1 x pink and white calico scallop seashell
- 1 x green turbo shell
- 12 in. (30.5 cm) driftwood branch

TOOLS AND MATERIALS
- funnel
- 12 in. (30.5 cm) transparent monofilament cord
- scissors

1. Create drainage and filtration layers. Layer the bottom of the container with a handful of river rocks to allow for drainage. Next, add 1 cup (240 ml) of gravel. Use scissors to cut the fiberglass screen sheet into a circle roughly 1 in. (2.5 cm) in diameter smaller than the inside of your container. Position the screen mesh in the center of your terrarium. The screen mesh prevents charcoal and soil from falling through to the next layer and helps filter the water for your terrarium. Pour horticultural charcoal over the screen mesh.

2. Add a substrate layer and plants. Fill in another layer of gravel around the inside edge of the terrarium to keep the screen mesh in place. Funnel succulent soil mix into the terrarium. Use the screen mesh as a guide, and do not let any soil get beyond the edge of the mesh or it will be seen through the glass. Place the plants inside the terrarium, with the tallest ones (the jade varieties) in the back and the crinkle-leaf in front. Add the remaining soil to cover the roots and press it down firmly to keep the plants in place.

3. Add a decorative layer. Pour in the remaining gravel until all of the soil is completely covered and then place your decorative shells inside the terrarium.

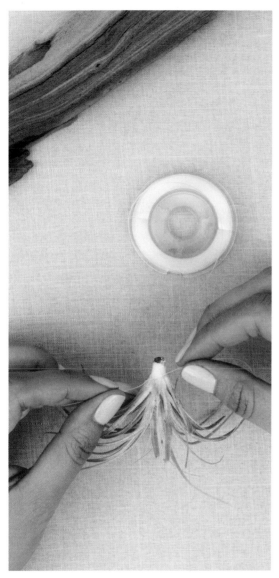

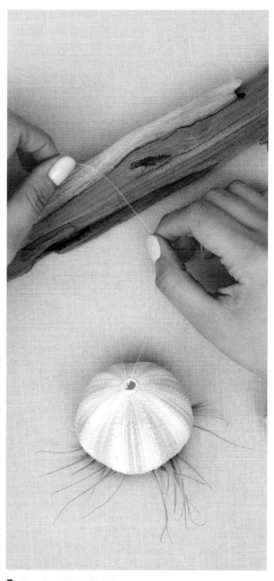

4. Attach the air plant to the sea urchin. Take one end of the transparent cord and tie a double knot around the base of several air plant leaves (closest to the root). This will not harm the air plant as long as you don't make the knot too tight. Most sea urchins come with a large opening on the underside and a small opening on top. Thread your cord through the large opening (underside) and out through the small opening on top. The urchin shell should fit snugly around the root of your air plant much like a hat. Your "jellyfish" is complete.

5. Tie the "jellyfish" to the driftwood. The length you chose to cut your cord depends on the height of your container. Your jellyfish should hang at least 4 inches (10 cm) above the plants. This will give them room to grow. Lastly, lay the driftwood branch over the top of your container.

JAR-RY RIGGED

THIS LITTLE LIGHT OF MINE

Upcycle an ordinary mason jar into a terrarium lamp for your side table or nightstand. A functional terrarium lamp is a great way to add a touch of nature indoors without compromising precious counter space. Mason jar lamp kits are readily available for purchase from large box stores or online home décor stores—no assembly necessary! Simply create a mini garden inside a mason jar, screw the lid on tightly, plug the extension into the wall, and voilà!

Selaginella kraussiana is a verdant, low-growing tropical plant that thrives in high humidity, making it the perfect choice for this closed mason jar terrarium. For a modern look, we'll use a neutral color palette for our layering ingredients.

VESSEL
- 64 oz. (2 L) wide-mouth mason jar

FOUNDATION
- ¼ cup (60 mL) black sand
- ¼ cup (60 mL) white sand
- ¼ cup (60 mL) beige sand
- 1 cup (240 mL) white river pebbles
- ½ cup (120 mL) sphagnum moss
- 1½ cups (350 mL) peat moss soil mix

PLANTS
- *Selaginella kraussiana* Spreading Club Moss

TOOLS AND MATERIALS
- wide-mouth mason jar lamp kit
- light bulb (light kit will specify light bulb size)
- funnel
- flattening tool (bamboo skewer and cork)
- long tweezers (optional)
- squeeze bottle with narrow nozzle

1. Create a decorative sand layer. Use a funnel to pour sand into the bottom of the jar, alternating between beige, white, and black layers. To get even layers, give the jar a gentle shake after adding each layer.

2. Create a drainage layer. Using your hands, drop white river pebbles into the jar.

3. Add the sphagnum moss layer. Cover the white river rocks with sphagnum moss. Use a flattening tool to flatten the moss completely. It is not necessary, but it does create a cleaner, more manicured appearance.

4. Add a filtration Layer. Drop in horticultural charcoal until the moss is completely covered. This layer will help filter the water and keep your terrarium free from mold.

5. Add peat moss soil mix and the plants. Use a cup or your hands to add the peat moss soil mix to the jar. Then remove the *Selaginella kraussiana* from its pot and transfer it to the jar. Depending on the size of your pot, you may find an extensive root system underneath. Use long tweezers or a bamboo skewer to help you position the roots inside the jar.

6. Wash down the sides of the jar and add water. Use a squeeze bottle to wash down the sides of the jar. Add ¼ cup (60 mL) of water to kick-start the water cycle.

TERRARIUM CARE

All plants need a rest period from light, and this project is no different. Place your terrarium in a shaded area and always keep the soil moist. For the most part this is a self-sustaining ecosystem. Keep in mind that if your lid is not airtight you may occasionally need to add more water.

7. Add the light bulb and screw on the lid. Not all light kits come with a light bulb; check if yours does or not, and be sure to check the light bulb size recommendation on the label before purchasing. Screw the light bulb in place and twist the lid over the mason jar until it is tight. Plug the extension into a wall socket and enjoy your new lamp!

WILD THING

IT'S A JUNGLE OUT THERE

While a well-manicured terrarium is all well and good, not all terrarium plants need to be tamed. Like something out of the jungles of Costa Rica, this wild thing is free to grow as it pleases. And let's ditch the traditional layering techniques for a road-less-traveled look. Instead, you will layer the foundation with only charcoal, rocks, and potting soil. Since this scene breaks from the norm, you will also explore glass etching to etch a motto into the sides of the terrarium. You will fill it with some of the most popular and easy-to-find houseplants out there.

VESSEL
- 6 x 6 x 6 in. (15 x 15 x 15 cm) square glass vase

FOUNDATION
- 2 cups (475 mL) horticultural charcoal
- 3 cups (700 mL) blue river rocks
- 5 cups (1.2 L) potting soil mix

PLANTS
- 1 x *Syngonium podophyllum* 'White Butterfly'
- 1 x *Chamaedora elegans* Parlor Palm
- 1 x *Hypoestes phyllostachya* Polka Dot Plant
- 1 x *Fittonia albivenis* Nerve Plant
- 1 x *Asparagus densiflorus* 'Sprengeri' Asparagus Fern

DECORATIVE ELEMENTS
- 2 cups (475 mL) black river rocks
- lichen-covered branches

TOOLS AND MATERIALS
- painter's tape
- adhesive stencils
- latex gloves
- paintbrush
- glass-etching medium

1. Adhere stencils to the glass. Peel-and-stick stencils are available at most craft stores. Think about what you want to say, and then select word stencils or decorative designs—whatever you like! When you're ready to stencil, begin by peeling the stencils from the paper backing and placing them directly in the center of the glass. Stencils are very forgiving, and you can peel and reposition them as much as you like until the words are level. Use painter's tape to protect the glass from the etching medium. Leave only the stencil cutouts exposed.

2. Apply etching medium to the glass. Carefully read and follow the instructions on the bottle before using any glass-etching product because it is extremely potent stuff. And to prevent the solution from making any contact with your skin, I strongly suggest wearing latex gloves. Apply a thin layer of etching medium to the glass and use a paintbrush to spread the solution evenly over the stencils. After the solution has set (according to the instructions), you can wash it off under running water. Pat dry with paper towel and peel away the stencils. Stencils are reusable, so you can repeat these steps on each side of the square vessel.

3. Add a drainage layer. Add an even layer of horticultural charcoal.

4. Add rocks. Follow the charcoal with a layer of river rocks about 1 in. (2.5 cm) deep.

5. Add more charcoal and potting mix. Before adding the soil mix, add another thin layer of charcoal to help prevent mold and keep the terrarium fresh. Pour potting soil mix over the charcoal. To add a little extra height to the plants, add extra soil to the back right corner of the container.

6. Remove plants from their pots and plant them in the terrarium. You may wish to wear gardening gloves for this step; it's up to you. First, plant small plants in the front, followed by the taller plants in the back. This will give you more room to work. To remove a plant from its pot, place one hand around the base of the plant, and with the other hand, wiggle the pot away from the plant. If the pot won't budge you can loosen the inside edges of the pot with a bamboo skewer. Once the plant is free, massage the root ball to remove any excess soil. Make a small well in the soil and drop the plant in. Firmly cover the roots with soil. Repeat these steps until all plants have been planted.

7. Add topdressing and decorative elements. For topdressing, use black river stones to cover the soil. For a real jungle vibe, add bits of branches covered in lichen around the front of the terrarium. In the back, add larger branches in a vertical position so they stand above the taller plants.

THE BEADS' KNEES

Air plants require very little care and like hanging out pretty much anywhere near a light source. In this project, transform your ordinary desk organizer into a dreamy deskscape terrarium. In lieu of rocks and soil, you'll use decorative beads and fancy glass chips for an added pop of color. Complete the look with a touch of colored moss, and voilà! A vibrant dwelling for your new desktop companions.

VESSEL
- glass desk organizer with multiple compartments

PLANTS
- 1 x *Tillandsia araujei* 'Purple Star'
- 1 x *Tillandsia ionantha* Guatemala
- 1 x *Tillandsia stricta* (fine leaf)

DECORATIVE ELEMENTS
- 3 strands of pink fashion beads in different sizes
- 2 cups (475 mL) pink crushed glass chips
- preserved black reindeer moss
- purple Spanish moss
- office supplies

TOOLS AND MATERIALS
- spoon

1. Mix decorative glass and beads. In a small bowl, sprinkle in your glass chips and beads and mix them together. Spoon the glass and bead mix into the desk organizer compartments—I filled the two largest compartments, but you can do whatever works best for the container you have on hand.

2. Add moss. For added height, place a small clump of black reindeer moss over the glass and bead mix.

3. Make an air plant nest. To form a nest for your 'Purple Star' to perch on, take the purple Spanish moss in one hand and circle it around your index and middle fingers two to three times, twisting as you go along, until you form a mini nest.

4. Add air plants. Position the Spanish moss nest over the black moss so that a touch of black moss is still visible. Place the 'Purple Star' in the center of the Spanish moss nest, and the Guatemala in a different compartment. Finally, fill your desk organizer with colorful stationery or fun office supplies.

TERRARIUM CARE

Air plants appreciate a hint of humidity. As an added treat, mist your plants once a week. Misting will not make up for watering, so continue to keep your air plants hydrated by submerging them in water for 20 minutes once a week.

ORCHID MANIA

TROPICAL PARADISE UNDER GLASS

When Europeans first discovered orchids in the 19th century, it sent them into *orchidarium* (orchid mania). Similar to fern fever, wealthy patrons sponsored orchid expeditions all over the world. "Orchid hunter" became an official job title! The most famous gardener-turned-orchid hunter was Benedict Roezl. Hunting for orchids meant Roezl had to sail across oceans, scale mountains, traverse jungles, evade hostile animals, and fight off tropical diseases. On one expedition to the Philippines, a man in his party was reportedly devoured by a tiger. So you can imagine how good Roezl was at his job by managing to collect over 800 captivating orchid species. In retrospect, it all makes hunting for orchids at the local garden center seem unadventurous . . . not that I'm complaining about the lack of tigers!

Today there are thousands of orchid species, and serious collectors are no less entranced by them. Case in point, in 2005, the Shenzhen Nongke orchid was created by scientists and sold at auction for almost a quarter million dollars. Fortunately for us, we don't all have to spend a fortune to own one of these beauties. I purchased the one in this project for less than $10 from my local Trader Joe's.

Being the tropical plants that they are, many orchids are right at home in terrariums. In this scene, the orchid takes center stage, with a colorful *Cryptanthus* Earth Star by its side. Moss is an orchid's best friend, and, on the flip side, I added an agate geode for a hint of glitz.

VESSEL
- 24 x 22 in. (60 x 55 cm) glass vase with lid

FOUNDATION
- 2 cups (475 mL) purple aquarium gravel
- sphagnum moss
- horticultural charcoal
- potting soil
- orchid bark

PLANTS
- 1 x *Phalaenopsis* Moth Orchid
- 1 x *Cryptanthus* Earth Star
- 10 x *Leucobryum glaucum* Pincushion Moss

DECORATIVE ELEMENTS
- purple and green preserved Spanish moss
- large river rocks
- artificial butterfly
- plant clip (this should come attached to the plant stake when you purchase an orchid)

TOOLS AND MATERIALS
- chopstick or long spoon
- scissors
- hot glue gun and glue sticks
- gardening gloves (optional)
- squeeze bottle with narrow nozzle

BEFORE YOU BEGIN

Rinse aquarium gravel and rocks under running water. Allow to air dry before assembling terrarium.

1. Create a drainage layer. Fill the bottom of the vessel with purple aquarium gravel to a depth of 1 in. (2.5 cm). You will use two different soil mediums in this terrarium. To keep them separate, create a barrier using decorative rocks. Line the rocks down the center of the vessel and around the inside edge of the terrarium. This will also keep the soil hidden from view.

2. Add a filtration layer. Spread sphagnum moss over the aquarium gravel and on both sides of the barrier. Next, cover the moss with a thin layer of horticultural charcoal.

3. Create a bromeliad substrate layer. Add potting soil to one side of the barrier. Fill to about 2 in. (5 cm) deep and then use a chopstick or long spoon to create a well for your *Cryptanthus* to be planted into.

4. Add green moss and your first plant. Place 6 pieces of pincushion moss side by side on top of the soil and decorative rocks. Allow some space between the moss and the glass. Lower down your *Cryptanthus* and firmly plant the roots into the soil. I like to tilt it slightly toward the glass to get a better view of this colorful star. Add the remaining pincushion moss around the backside of the bromeliad.

5. Create an orchid substrate layer. Turn the vessel to begin working on the backside of the terrarium, where your orchid will live. Orchids love moisture, but not wet roots. To help with drainage, add a layer of orchid bark over the charcoal and sphagnum moss. Orchid bark does not absorb water and prevents orchid roots from getting too soggy.

6. Unpot the orchid. An orchid generally comes in a decorative pot and plastic cup. Remove it from its decorative pot and cut away the plastic cup with a pair of scissors. Be careful not to damage any roots while cutting. This orchid was planted in sphagnum moss. It can be directly dropped into a terrarium without any need for soil.

DID YOU KNOW?

Orchids have roots that grow above the surface of the soil. They are called "air roots," and they look shiny and bluish in color. It's a common misconception that air roots signal the need to repot an orchid. In fact, air roots help collect moisture and carbon dioxide for photosynthesis. When planting orchids, allow air roots to freely float above the surface.

TERRARIUM CARE

Place the terrarium in a place with indirect sunlight. Direct sunlight may cause both plants to burn. If you notice water droplets forming on the glass, this is a sign of too much moisture. Take the lid off for a few hours to let some of the moisture evaporate.

7. Add a decorative butterfly. Most orchids come with a plant stake and clip to help it stay upright. Remove the stake and plastic clip. Hot glue a decorative butterfly to one side of the clip. Allow the glue to dry (about 10 minutes) before clipping the butterfly to the stem of the orchid. If your orchid needs additional support add the plant stake into the terrarium. I personally like the look without it.

8. Add the orchid, decorative elements, and water. Lower the orchid into the terrarium where it can live snugly between the Spanish moss and *cryptanthus*. Then place an agate geode at the base of the orchid. Before you place the lid on your terrarium, fill a squeeze bottle with 4 oz. of water and wash down the sides of the terrarium.

WOODLAND CHANDELIER

I'VE TAKEN A LICHEN TO MOSS

I confess, I'm a city girl, through and through—partly because I've never known anything different and partly because I need Starbucks to be within walking distance of me at all times. So that one time my husband told me he was taking me camping, I sort of laughed. Outside? Bugs? Bears!? No way! It wasn't until we bought a portable grill that I got a tad excited (I'll go anywhere if there's food). Two weeks later, we were in the woods, and once I got over my insect anxiety, I was having the time of my life. Being outside in the fresh air with all of the trees and plants gave me a sense of calm that I've never felt before. By that same token, just a little green in every corner of my home never fails to give me that same relaxed, feel-good effect.

In this project, we are bringing the outdoors inside. If you struggle with keeping plants alive due to low-light conditions, or you don't have time for maintenance, you'll love this mossy terrarium. You will use several different types of preserved moss and a faux fern garland so that the chandelier stays looking vibrant all year long.

VESSELS
- 6 x 3 x 5 in. (7.5 x 12.5 cm) glass light bulb terrariums

FOUNDATION
- decorative gold rocks

PLANTS
- white and mint green reindeer moss
- emerald green preserved Spanish moss

DECORATIVE ELEMENTS
- branch with lichen and moss
- red pine bark

- 7 yd. (6.5 m) silk cord—brown
- 6 ft. (1.8 m) faux maidenhair fern garland
- 12 in. (30.5 cm) gold metal hoop
- 2 in. (5 cm) round metal gold ring

TOOLS AND MATERIALS
- floral wire
- scissors
- wire cutters
- measuring tape
- craft glue or hot glue gun with glue sticks (optional)
- ceiling hook

1. Prep your set of 6 light bulb terrariums. Cut 6 pieces of cord according to the following lengths: 6 in. (15 cm), 9 in. (23 cm), 12 in. (30.5 cm), 15 in. (38 cm), 18 in. (45.5 cm), and 21 in. (53 cm). Each light bulb has a small hole at the top. Beginning with the smallest cord, string one end through the top and out through the small cutout opening in the front, and then make a double knot to secure that end. Repeat these steps for each cord length and terrarium. Note: some cords may be more "slippery" than others. Depending on the cord you use, you may want to add a dab of craft glue or hot glue to hold the knot in place and keep it from coming undone.

2. Add rocks and branches. To give that "illuminated" look, I used small gold decorative rocks that reflect the light. Add moss and decorative elements such as small twigs, lichen, and moss. If you have a large branch, break off two to three small pieces to fit inside each terrarium. To add some height to the design, position them vertically in the center of the light bulb. Conveniently, you can order branches covered in lichen and moss online.

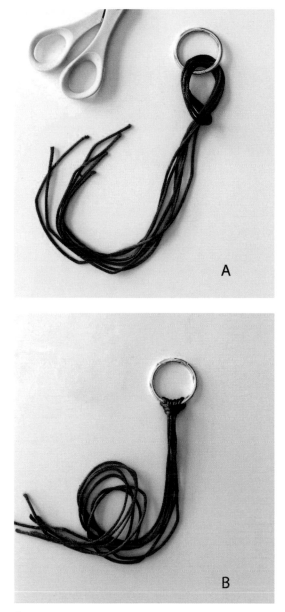

3. Add moss and bark. Nestle small bits of emerald green Spanish moss around the twigs and around the sides. Spanish moss can be unruly, so I like to roll the moss in the palms of my hands to give it a rounder shape before placing inside the terrarium. Tear off small pieces of mint green and white reindeer moss and add them inside as well. Lastly, break off small pieces of bark and place them around the opening of the terrarium. Repeat the same steps for all 6 light bulb terrariums.

4. Measure and cut cord for the mobile. Cut 3 pieces of cord, each 20 in. (50 cm) in length. Gather all three and fold in half so that you have 6 strands, each 10 in. (25.5 cm) in length. Next, you will make a lark's knot. Take your loop and bring it behind and then through the center of the gold ring (Figure A). Pull the strands through the center of the loop and then pull the strands downward to tighten the knot (Figure B).

6. Attach the terrariums to the hoop. Because we want the light bulbs to hang in a spiral, we need to tie each light bulb to the hoop in ascending order. Begin with the shortest cord and work your way around the hoop until all cords are equally spaced out and tied with a double knot.

5. Tie the ends of each cord to the large gold hoop. Equally space out each strand before tying it with a double knot. If you think the knots will come undone, add a bit of glue to each knot.

BRIGHT IDEA!

Faux garlands not your thing? Substitute faux ferns with fresh-cut eucalyptus leaves, boxwood leaves, or even olive branches. Check out etsy.com for fresh-cut garlands delivered straight to your door!

7. Attach garland. This is my favorite part, and way easier than it looks! Line up the faux maidenhair fern garland with the gold hoop and use floral wire to secure the garland all the way around the hoop. Wind the floral wire around the garland and hoop a couple of times and use wire cutters to snip off the wire. Tuck the remaining wire into the garland. Hang it from a ceiling hook in a dark corner or other area of your home to brighten it up a bit!

ZEN SUCCULENCE

MILLENNIAL ZEN GARDEN

Mini Japanese Zen gardens are making a huge comeback, but this one has a twist—the plant pot levitates and slowly spins so you can admire the plant from all sides! This mini garden is the ultimate indulgence for any nature-loving tech junkie. The levitating kit comes with a magnetic base that lights up, and a complementary bamboo pot to plant a jade plant or even miniature bonsai. Decorate with simple gravel and modest mood moss for a truly Zen aesthetic.

VESSEL
- 12 x 8 x 2 in. (30 x 20 x 5 cm) accessory tray (white)

FOUNDATION
- ½ cup (120 mL) succulent soil mix
- 1½ cups (350 mL) peat moss soil mix

PLANTS
- 1 x *Crassula ovata* 'Obliqua' Jade Plant
- 1 x clump *Dicranum scoparium* Mood Moss

DECORATIVE ELEMENTS
- small dried tree branch
- beige aquarium gravel

TOOLS AND MATERIALS
- levitating bamboo plant pot with magnetic base
- plastic lining (you could also use a plastic magazine sleeve)
- marker
- painter's tape
- drill with drill bit (drill bit can vary, depending on the pot's power cord)

1. Mark where you will drill. Position the magnetic base inside the tray with the port facing the side of the tray where the power cord will be threaded through and connected to the port. Place a piece of painter's tape where you will drill, and mark an X on the spot with a marker. Remove the magnetic base and get your drill ready.

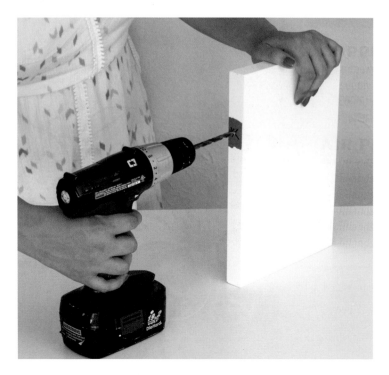

2. Drill a hole into the tray. Depending on the size of power cord that comes with your levitation kit, you will need to select the appropriate drill bit size (I used a ¼ in. [6 mm] drill bit). Drill a hole all the way through the side of the tray.

3. Add a base layer. To protect the tray, line the bottom with a sheet of plastic. Next, add an even layer of gravel. Place the base of the pot on the tray (be sure to line up the port with the hole you drilled.

4. Add the foundation. To divide and contain the foundation, place a dried branch or driftwood in the tray, diagonally. Fill the space behind the branch with peat moss.

5. Fill the tray with gravel and moss. Place mood moss over peat moss soil and press it down firmly to remove any air pockets. Fill the tray with more gravel. Feed the power cord through the port and plug it into the base. Plug the other end into the wall.

6. Add succulents to the magnetic plant pot. Since succulents don't like soggy feet, add a layer of small pebbles to the bottom of the pot to help with drainage. Fill the pot with succulent soil mix and plant your succulents. Turn on the levitating base and very slowly line up the magnetic pot with the base. Once in place, the pot levitates and spins in place.

TERRARIUM CARE

Mist mood moss several times a week to keep it green. Remove the levitating pot once a week and thoroughly water the succulents.

TEST SUBJECTS

INDULGE YOUR INNER PLANT SCIENTIST

Have you ever heard of plant swapping? Informally, it's been going on forever. It's when friends and neighbors gift each other plants to grow their burgeoning gardens. Lately, however, a new generation of plant enthusiasts is raising the stakes, organizing events that are popping up all over! At these plant parties, everyone involved brings cuttings or seeds to trade for something new to take home. Once you bring home your new seeds or cuttings, you of course must find new and unexpected ways to display them—it's all part of being a plant parent!

I'm always on the lookout for unique glass vessels, and since terrariums are not far from science experiments, this test tube display caught my eye. Test tubes make the perfect homes for seedlings or cuttings. Fill each test tube with eye-catching layers, plant seeds or plant cuttings, and watch them grow!

VESSEL
- brass and clear glass test tube vases

FOUNDATION
- palm and cactus soil mix

PLANT CUTTINGS
- 1 x *Echeveria subsessilis* 'Morning Beauty'
- 1 x *Chamaedora elegans* Parlor Palm
- 1 x *Echeveria* 'Tulip'
- 1 x *Senecio rowleyanus* String of Pearls
- 1 x *Echeveria setosa* v. *oteroi*

DECORATIVE ELEMENTS
- silver decorative rocks
- crushed blue glass
- white sand
- blue reindeer moss

TOOLS AND MATERIALS
- bamboo skewer or wood dowel
- spoon
- funnel

BEFORE YOU BEGIN

Wash the river rocks with warm, soapy water and allow them to dry completely before use.

1. Layer sand and crushed glass. Use a funnel to spoon one spoonful of black sand, followed by one spoonful of crushed blue glass, into each test tube.

2. Add sand and rocks to make the second layer. Funnel one spoonful of white sand and one of silver rocks into each test tube.

TERRARIUM CARE

The Parlor Palm requires slightly different conditions than the succulents. Keep the soil evenly moist at all times. Succulents only need to be watered thoroughly once a week.

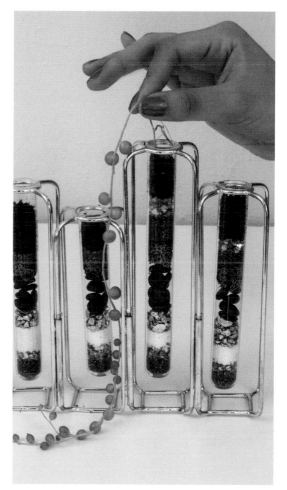

3. Layer moss and river pebbles. Your river pebbles may not fit into the funnel, so you will need to drop them into each test tube. You can eyeball it and fill to a depth of about 1 in. (2.5 cm). Tear small pieces of blue reindeer moss and use a bamboo skewer to press them down into the test tubes. Some test tubes are shorter than others, so, at this point, you can leave some as they are or add another layer of crushed glass and black sand before adding the soil.

4. Add soil and plants. Use the funnel and spoon to add at least 1 in. (2.5 cm) of soil to each test tube. You can use the bamboo skewer to make a small well in the soil for your cuttings to be placed into. Once the stems are in the soil, you may need to top off with a little extra soil.

SECRET GARDEN

SERIOUS BUNNY BUSINESS

By now you are familiar with succulents and their need for well-draining soil. As a general guideline, houseplants prefer soil that retains a little more moisture than their desert counterparts, hence it is rare to find houseplants living alongside succulents in a terrarium. Enter the *Plectranthus tomentosa*. This unique succulent looks much like a houseplant. However, like most succulents, it doesn't mind dry soil between waterings. With its minty leaves, it is affectionately referred to as the "Vicks Plant." Kids especially can't resist the urge to run their fingers over the furry green leaves (well, neither can I, for that matter). Complete with pastel succulents and miniature bunnies deep in conversation, this project is fun for kids of all ages.

VESSEL
- 8.25 in. high x 10 in. diameter (21 cm high x 25 cm diameter) glass bubble bowl

FOUNDATION
- 1½ cups (350 mL) white rocks
- 2 cups (475 mL) sphagnum moss
- 3 cups (700 mL) succulent soil mix
- 1½ cups (350 mL) horticultural charcoal

PLANTS
- 3 x *Echeveria* 'Perle von Nurnberg'
- 1 x *Plectranthus tomentosa* Vicks Plant
- 1 x *Echeveria* 'Emerald Ripple'
- 1 x *Echeveria* 'Melaco'
- 1 x *Echeveria secunda* v. glauca

DECORATIVE ELEMENTS
- 2 x miniature bunny figurines
- 2 x pyrite (fool's gold) nuggets
- 2 x black river rocks
- 1½ cups (350 mL) mixed marble rocks
- green reindeer moss

TOOLS AND MATERIALS
- tweezers
- E6000 glue
- flattening tool (bamboo skewer and cork)

BEFORE YOU BEGIN

Rinse rocks under running water. Allow them to air dry before assembling terrarium.

1. Create the drainage layer. You are going to use the drainage layer to create a slope to give the scene more dimension. First, fill the bottom of the bowl with white rocks to a depth of 2 in. (5 cm). Tilt the bowl back so that the rocks slide back and sit higher up than the ones in the front. Fill in any gaps with more rocks.

2. Add a filtration layer. Add a layer of sphagnum moss about 1 in. (2.5cm) deep and then sprinkle in ½ cup (120 mL) of horticultural charcoal over the moss.

3. Create a substrate layer.
Pour well-draining succulent soil mix into the terrarium and use your flattening tool to even out the foreground, where your rocks and miniatures will be displayed.

4. Add plants.
Place the smallest plants inside the terrarium first. Plant each succulent side by side near the center of the vessel but leave room for the bunny scene in the front. Plant the tallest plant (*Plectranthus tomentosa*) last.

5. Add topdressing. Add marble rocks to the terrarium. You can use a bamboo skewer to sweep the pebbles all around the succulents and under their leaves until the soil is covered. Add 2 large black pebbles side by side near the front of the vessel. This is where your bunnies will sit.

6. Add decorative elements. As the scene fills up, long tweezers will come in handy. Position moss and pyrite stones along the inner edge of the vessel. Add pieces of brightly colored moss between succulents and rocks.

7. Glue the bunnies to the black river rocks. Add a drop of E6000 glue to the underside of each bunny. Use tweezers to hold the figurines in place until the glue is dry. Alternatively, you can use Super Glue. I would not suggest using hot glue, as it does not hold up to water very well.

TERRARIUM CARE

Water plants once a week with 4-6 oz. (120–175 mL) of water. I like to use a squeeze bottle with a narrow nozzle so I can water just the base of each plant. Avoid getting water on the reindeer moss, or it will get stiff and the color will begin to fade. Occasionally, you may need to trim the *Plectranthus tomentosa* to keep it confined to the terrarium. Set the terrarium in a place with lots of sunlight, like near a south-facing window.

FOUR EASY WAYS TO STYLE AIR PLANTS

I really can't remember when I saw air plants for the first time, but I do remember the first time they left a dramatic impression on me. I was perusing an incredible store devoted to plants and oddities of all kinds, and there, between the framed butterflies and a scene of Victorian-dressed, taxidermy mice having tea, I found a beautiful selection of air plants. The "leggy" sort (*Tillandsia caput-medusae*) was suspended from above in what looked like a troupe of ballerinas dancing through the air. In complete contrast, the "hairy" variety (*Tillandsia tectorum*) appeared disheveled, on the verge of stumbling drunkenly out of apothecary jars and containers.

This was the first time I really appreciated air plants for all their charisma and versatility. Not only do they all have their own personalities, they can also be hung from a ceiling, burrowed between books on a shelf, or naturally allowed to cling to any number of decorative objects around your house. If you let your imagination run wild, you will have endless fun designing your air plant terrariums and finding new places for them to dwell. Here are a few ideas to get you started!

SERVING DISH

SUPPLIES
- serving dish
- purple sand

AIR PLANTS
- 1 x *Tillandsia Ionantha rubra*
- 1 x *Tillandsia brachycaulos × abdita*
- 1 x *Tillandsia Ionantha scaposa*

DECORATIVE ELEMENTS
- 2 x white quartz crystals
- 1 x amethyst crystal
- 1 x citrine crystal

1. Wash the serving dish with warm, soapy water and let dry completely.

2. Pour the sand into the serving dish until you have a hill in the center.

3. Press the crystals and air plants into the sand, alternating between the two.

STEMMED GLASS

SUPPLIES
- snifter (any stemmed glass will do!)

AIR PLANTS
- 1 x *Tillandsia filifolia*

DECORATIVE ELEMENTS
- monochrome aquarium gravel mix

1. Wash the glass with warm, soapy water and let dry completely.

2. Fill the bottom of the glass with a thin layer of aquarium gravel.

3. Place the air plant inside.

GRAPEWOOD VINE

SUPPLIES
- grapewood vine (available from floral supply shops)
- E6000 glue
- rubber bands (optional)

AIR PLANTS
- *Tillandsia ionantha rubra*
- *Tillandsia ionantha scaposa*
- *Tillandsia caput-medusae*
- *Tillandsia harrisii*
- *Tillandsia filifolia*
- *Tillandsia xerographica*

1. Apply a small amount of E6000 glue to the vine where you would like the air plants to sit.

2. Simply nestle the *xerographica* between branches. There is no need to glue this one.

CRYSTALS

SUPPLIES
- E6000 glue
- rubber bands (optional)

AIR PLANTS
- *Tillandsia ionantha rubra*
- *Tillandsia ionantha scaposa*
- *Tillandsia caput-medusae*
- *Tillandsia harrisii*
- *Tillandsia filifolia*
- *Tillandsia xerographica*

1. Wash crystals in warm, soapy water and let them dry.

2. Add a small amount of glue to the crystal where you would like the air plant to sit. Wait a few minutes for the glue to get tacky.

3. Press the air plant into the glue and hold down until the glue dries (about 10 minutes). Repeat for the other crystals/air plants.

CARE

Place air plant displays in bright rooms with indirect sunlight. If your air plants are glued down, mist them every other day. Avoid letting too much water get into the bases. Air plants that are not glued down can be removed from their display once a week and submerged in a bowl of water for 20 minutes. Remove them from their bath, shake out any excess water, and allow them to dry upside down before returning them to their display.

CAPTURE THE RAINBOW

WITHOUT THE RAIN THERE WOULD BE NO RAINBOW

There's nothing quite like seeing a rainbow after the rain. Bursting across the sky with beautiful colors, it always reminds me that there is so much magic in this world. While that pot of gold eludes me every time (darn you, leprechauns!), I'll chase a rainbow any day!

In this terrarium scene, we're going to capture our own rainbow and keep it in a stemmed glass for all to admire. I've always been a fan of snow globes, so let's use white sand as topdressing which really makes the pretty pastels and green succulents pop. Lastly, no rainbow is complete without a couple of golden nuggets!

VESSEL
- 8 x 10 in. (20 x 25 cm) large stemmed glass

FOUNDATION
- 2 cups (475 mL) white sand
- 2 cups (475 mL) marble pebbles
- fiberglass screen sheet
- 2 cups (475 mL) potting soil
- ½ cup (120 mL) horticultural charcoal

PLANTS
- 2 x *Asparagus densiflorus* 'Sprengeri' Asparagus Fern
- 2 x *Selaginella kraussiana* 'Brownii" Pincushion Spike Moss
- 1 x *Anacampseros telephiastrum variegata* 'Sunrise'—top cutting only

DECORATIVE ELEMENTS
- reindeer moss in green, purple, orange, and pink
- preserved sheet moss
- pine bark
- 2 x pyrite (fool's gold) nuggets
- jewelry wire in green, violet, blue, gold, and red

TOOLS AND MATERIALS
- flattening tool (bamboo skewer and cork)
- wire cutters
- scissors
- ruler
- funnel

1. Create a drainage layer. Pour marble rocks into the bottom of the vessel.

2. Add the separation and foundation layers. Roughly cut a sheet of fiberglass screen to fit over the drainage layer. Add horticultural charcoal over the separation screen.

3. Add a substrate layer. Add potting mix to the vessel. Even out the soil by pressing down on the soil with your flattening tool. Next, make small pockets in the soil with the other end of the bamboo skewer or your finger.

4. Add your plants. Add the asparagus ferns to both sides of the vessel. Follow by placing a *Selaginella kraussiana* in front of each fern. Fully cover the roots with soil.

5. Add topdressing. Top the soil with white sand using a funnel. Keep the tip of the funnel low while you are pouring the sand so the sand powder does not cloud the inside of the vessel. Now, flip the terrarium around to work on the backside.

6. Add preserved sheet moss. Cut a piece of preserved sheet moss in the shape of a trapezoid, with the longest side closest to the back of the terrarium. This will help break up the sand and woodland scene.

7. Add pine bark. Place a piece of pine bark over the moss. Now your woodsy scene is coming to life!

8. Add moss. Place colorful moss behind the pine bark and around the inside of the terrarium.

9. Add succulents and decorative elements. It's rare for ferns and succulents to share the same terrarium. But I have an easy trick! You can always take stem cuttings from succulents and use them to decorate any open-vessel terrarium. They go best near the front of the terrarium. Place colorful purple, orange, and pink reindeer moss in a small mound near the front. Take a cutting of *Anacampseros telephiastrum* and press the stem into the colorful bed of moss. The succulent can stay in the display for up to two months while it grows roots. Once roots are fully formed, you can plant it in a pot or new terrarium with other succulents. Next, add additional bits of moss throughout and your little gold nuggets.

TERRARIUM CARE

Medium light will do right by this terrarium. Use a squeeze bottle with a narrow nozzle to water your plants once a week and lightly mist the *Selaginella kraussiana* once a week.

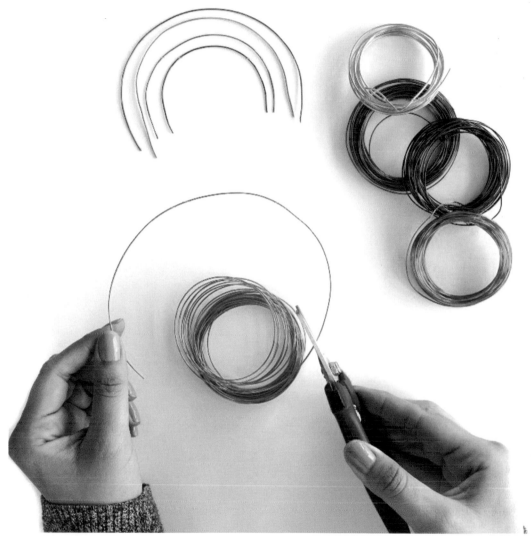

10. Use colored wire to create a rainbow. I like buying wire rounds because, when you unwind one, it's already shaped like an arch, so there is no need to bend it into the shape we need for the rainbow. Slightly unwind each wire (you can use a ruler to measure the length you need) and cut three of each color in the following sizes: red, 10 in. (25.5 cm); gold, 9 in. (23 cm); green, 8 in. (20 cm); blue, 7 in. (18 cm); and violet, 6 in. (15 cm). To assemble the rainbow, press both ends of each wire into the sand from shortest to longest wire. The order of colors is violet, blue, green, gold, red. Start with your three violet wires, and so on, until you finish with red. Add additional bits of moss and pyrite to finish.

PART 3:
KEEPING UP WITH
YOUR PLANTS

PEST CONTROL

FOR EVERY HERO, THERE'S A VILLAIN

At some point on your terrarium-making journey, you may come across some uninvited guests looking for a free meal. There are a bunch of ways that pests can make their way into your terrarium, from hitching a ride on a plant, to coming inside from an open window. It's natural for some insects to be attracted to the foliage inside your terrarium. However, some are more destructive than others; I outline a few of those here. If you notice an infestation, the first thing to do is to quarantine the affected plant so its neighbors do not come under siege. Uproot the plant from the terrarium using tweezers or chopsticks. Discard the affected soil, repot the plant in fresh soil, and begin the extermination process. Sorry to be the bearer of bad news, but if the infestation is extensive, you may need to discard the plant entirely. If you think you can salvage some healthy parts, take cuttings and repot those until you can reintroduce into a terrarium.

Mealybugs is their name, and annoying you to no end is their game. These ugly little critters love to take up residence on the surface and stems of cacti and succulents. In vampire fashion, they sink their sharp

OPTIONS FOR EXTERMINATING APHIDS AND MEALYBUGS

A hungry aphid

- **Running water.** Flush out the bugs by running the plant under a steady stream from the faucet. You may need to do this more than once. This option only works for succulents or plants that are still hardy. If the plant is too sickly, this option may further damage leaves.

- **Rubbing alcohol swabs.** Dip a cotton swab in rubbing alcohol and wipe away the bugs. Repeat every day until all the bugs are eliminated. This is a gentle approach to dealing with bug pests but could be time consuming.

- **Tape dab.** Apply double-sided tape to your index finger and wipe insects from leaves and stems. They will stick to the tape, so you can easily remove the tape from your finger and dispose of them.

- **Soap spray.** Mix together 1 tsp. (5 mL) pure castile liquid soap and 1 qt. (1 L) water. Fill a spray bottle with the mixture and spray only the area affected. Spray with water several hours later to remove any soap from the leaves. If necessary, repeat after two days.

TIPS ON HOW TO AVOID UNWANTED CRITTERS

- **Thoroughly examine all plants for pests before bringing them home** from a nursery or garden store and adding them to your collection. Check the undersides of leaves, between leaf joints, and the soil around the stem.

- **When planting soft succulents together in a terrarium, don't overcrowd them.** Leave a little bit of space between them for better air circulation. Additionally, in the event of an infestation, bugs will find it more difficult to colonize a neighboring plant. I admit, even I find this rule difficult to follow—sometimes I like to pack them all in like pickles!

- **Keep your terrarium clean and tidy.** Remove dried leaves as soon as possible. Dead leaves can lead to rotting and attract pests.

teeth into the soft tissue of succulents and feed on their sugary sap. I get itchy just thinking about it! Mealybugs are small, about ⅒ in. (2 mm), and so hard to spot. The white, webby substance they use to disguise themselves is good indication of an infestation. If you so much as see something that resembles a tiny ball of cotton, this is your cue to go into search-and-destroy mode. The plant will not survive if the bugs are not dealt with swiftly. Mealybugs move fast, so keep an eye on your other terrarium plants.

Aphids on the attack can be trouble because they reproduce rapidly. That is why it is important to catch them before too many set up shop. Similar to mealybugs, these menacing insects feed on plant sap with their needlelike mouths and can transmit viruses, causing plants to become

Mealybugs (*Pseudococcidae*) move fast, so keep an eye on your other terrarium plants!

Set a gnat trap! The gnats will be attracted to brightly colored paper, and, when they fly by for a closer look, they will get trapped.

sickly. There are several different aphid species, but most varieties find succulents and tropical plants to be a tasty treat! Aphids are about ⅛ in. (3mm), come in different colors, and like to grow their colonies on the undersides of leaves or near new growth. Plant symptoms include stunted growth, wilting, discoloration, and sticky mold fungus left behind by aphid secretion.

Fungus gnats are not as fun as their name implies. They are tiny, black, mosquito-like flies that like to feast on roots. They will immediately attack any new plant growth, so if you are propagating succulents or growing seedlings, fungus gnats will wreak havoc on them before they even have a chance to show you how pretty they are. Luckily, you can easily get rid of fungus gnats by making your own DIY gnat trap. Spread a thin layer of petroleum jelly on a brightly colored note

card and place the card on top of the soil in your terrarium. The gnats will be attracted to the brightly colored paper, and, when they fly by for a closer look, they will get trapped in the jelly. Leave the note card out until all of the gnats and second-generation larvae living in the soil are gone. This usually takes about three weeks.

Spider mites are mighty sapsuckers that like to hide on the undersides of leaves. They are so small (less than a millimeter) that you may not notice them until you discover a weblike substance between the stems and leaves of your plants. SNS 217 is an organic formula made from rosemary oil that, while nontoxic to people and animals, quickly kills spider mites and their eggs. Spray it on the undersides of leaves. One application is usually enough.

PROPAGATION

OFF WITH THEIR HEADS!

Sometimes in spite of our best efforts, terrarium plants will begin to get stretched out, or "leggy." The scientific name for this is *etiolation*. This is most common in succulents and happens when they lack proper sunlight. In a last-ditch effort to get more sunlight, their stems grow tall and their leaves become more spread out. It's really a shame when this occurs because they lose their natural shape and morph into something unrecognizable from their original appearance. The question on everyone's mind is always, "How can I stop my succulents from continuing to get leggy?" The simple answer is, you can't. Once they are stretched out, there is no putting Humpty Dumpty back together again. But have no fear! This is the perfect time to begin the propagation process.

Begin by popping off the lower leaves first. Hold the leaf between your thumb and index finger and wiggle left and right until it gives way. If you hear a slight popping sound, you know you've done it right. If any part of the leaf remains on the stem, the leaf will not be a viable candidate for propagation. Only those leaves cut cleanly from their bases will have a chance to grow roots.

Examples of bad (left), and good (right) leaf removal.

Continue popping leaves off until you get near the top of the stem. Collect your leaf cuttings and place them near a window for two to three days. This time allows the cuttings to callus over, which prevents bacteria from entering them. Next, place the leaves on a shallow bed of soil. I like to fill ramekins or shallow baking pans with soil and set the leaves down side by side. It's important to keep the soil moist but not drenched. Use a mister once a day to keep the soil evenly moist. You should begin seeing roots within one to two weeks and rosettes within three to four weeks. Eventually, the mother leaf will begin to shrivel and dry out. Feel free to cut off the mother leaf and plant your new succulent in a terrarium.

The next step in propagation is, for lack of a better word, decapitation! The top "bud" of the plant is generally all that remains of the succulent's original shape. The top can also be removed, allowed to grow new roots, and used in a new terrarium display. Take a pair of scissors or a sharp knife and cut the top off, about ½ inch (13 mm) below the last remaining leaf. You now have a succulent cutting. Allow the stem of the cutting to dry out near a window. After a few days, the cutting will be ready for a new terrarium home or living display.

Remember that leggy stem? Well, in the propagation process, no stem is left behind! Nothing goes to waste. Go back to the stem and cut it off near the base,

Examples of leaf propogation over a five-week time period.

leaving 1 inch (2.5 cm) of the stump. The stump will eventually regenerate and begin to grow one or more new baby rosettes. It also doesn't hurt to leave one or two leaves on the stump to help collect sunlight for the photosynthesis process to continue.

Propagation opens a whole new world of possibilities in terrarium making. Sometimes it *is* hard to find succulents that fit inside small glass vessels, which is why propagating your own succulents and taking small cuttings is a great way to have small succulents on hand when inspiration sparks. When it comes to succulent propagation, everyone has a slightly different method. It all depends on your climate and the amount of sunlight. If you live in a cold or dry climate, you may want to cover your cuttings with plastic wrap for the first few weeks to provide ample warmth and to keep the soil from drying out. You will be amazed at how much satisfaction you get from seeing one little leaf begin to sprout and become an entire garden. Try it out and see what works best for you!

After trimming the stem, the stump will eventually regenerate.

SOURCING
WHERE TO GET THE GOODS

TERRAIN	www.shopterrain.com	An excellent source for an inspiring collection of terrarium vessels, supplies, and accessories, including mossarium kits, reindeer moss, preserved sheet moss, orchid bark, decorative stones and marbles, soil mixes, faux succulents, misters, and an assorted collection of tropical plants and ferns.
SANDSATIONAL SPARKLE	www.sandsationalsparkle.com	The perfect source for colored sand in every color imaginable.
TARGET	www.target.com	An easy source for basic terrarium essentials, including glass vessels, decorative rocks, and potting mix.
MICHAELS	www.michaels.com	An excellent source for craft supplies and ready-to-use terrarium supplies including geometric glass vessels, faux succulents, river rocks, seashells, miniatures, glue, and colored sand.
MOUNTAIN CREST GARDENS	mountaincrestgardens.com	An amazing online source for purchasing succulents. Succulents are available for individual purchase, in sets, or in plug trays.
PISTILS NURSERY	pistilsnursery.com 3811 N. Mississippi Ave. Portland, Oregon	A beautiful storefront and online supplier of air plants, marimo balls, misters, crystals, and gemstones.
THE SILL	www.thesill.com 84 Hester St. at Allen St. New York, New York	An excellent source for small terrarium plants delivered straight to your door.
AIR PLANT SUPPLY CO.	www.airplantsupplyco.com	A great source for air plant vessels, tillandsias, and grapevine wood, among many other supplies.
COST PLUS WORLD MARKET	www.worldmarket.com	A gem when it comes to glass vessels and decorative rocks.
TERESA'S PLANTS	www.etsy.com/shop/ TeresasPlants	A great source for a wide variety of live moss and lichen. They also have an outstanding collection of decorative elements including shells, polished stones, crushed glass, gravel, and lichen-covered rocks.
THE CONTAINER STORE	www.containerstore.com	A great place to find terrarium vessels, including mason jars and canisters.
PETCO	www.petco.com	An excellent place to find colored gravel, sand, sphagnum moss, and marimo balls.
SUCCULENCE	www.thesucculence.com 402 Cortland Ave. Bernal Heights, San Francisco, California	An inspiring store filled to the brim with succulents, rare cacti, exotic air plants, and glass vessels. They offer classes and a planting bar where you can get down and dirty with your terrarium.
HOMEGOODS	www.homegoods.com	An excellent place to find unique glass vessels, including apothecary jars and vases.
HOBBY LOBBY	www.hobbylobby.com	The perfect source for glass terrarium vessels, decorative sand, funnels, crafting supplies, and realistic miniatures to help your mini world come to life.

ABOUT THE AUTHOR

@ @charmingproject

Enid G. Svymbersky is the creative blogger behind A Charming Project, a DIY style website where she shares her passion for plants and crafting. She first started crafting as a creative outlet, and soon became hooked on blogging when her Coffee Pot Terrarium project went viral. Between brunching and happy hour, you can usually find her planting, hot gluing, or painting her next project. Visit her online at *www.acharmingproject.com* and on Instagram at @charmingproject. Also on Facebook @acharmingproject.

ACKNOWLEDGMENTS

As I sit here and think of all the people who have helped me and supported me through this endeavor, I feel like the most fortunate person in the world. My heart will eternally be filled with love and gratitude for all of you!

A huge hug to all the folks at Fox Chapel Publishing who work hard to create books that inspire creativity in all of us. I especially want to acknowledge my editors: Bud Sperry for championing this book and lighting the way, and Jeremy Hauck for beautifully weaving my projects together.

To Igor (*www.happyinteriorblog.com*) and Judith (*www.joelix.com*) you are my inspiration! Thank you for bringing a global community of plant enthusiasts together in one place (*www.urbanjunglebloggers.com*). Without this platform, my projects would probably not have seen the light of day.

To my fellow Urban Jungle Bloggers, thank you for fighting for a greener world, one interior at a time!

To my husband, Michael: this book is as much yours as it is mine. You were there every step of the way, supporting me and pushing me to do more than I ever knew I could. Thank you for taking care of me while I was taking care of all our plant babies!

To Diane and Joe, a big hug to you guys for your love and encouraging words when I needed them the most.

To my brother, Xavier, for going above and beyond in every possible way. Thank you for being my photography assistant and for always keeping the coffee coming. You are tremendously talented, and I sincerely thank you for creating the wonderful illustrations in this book.

To my parents, Victor and Claudia, you are the hardest-working people I have ever known. Thank you for inspiring me, instilling your work ethic in me, and always nurturing my creativity. Your love and support will forever keep me pedaling big mountains.

And finally, a huge thank you to the readers of my blog, *A Charming Project*. Thank you for visiting and telling me stories of how you decorate parties with projects inspired by my blog! You have kept me going all these years, and I can't wait for us to share more stories and ideas together.

All photography by the author except for the below.
Shutterstock: 6 bottom left/New Africa, 6 top right/Madlen, 8/optimarc, 11/Jeerayut Rianwed, 13/White Space Ukraine, 14/3xy, 15/FireflyPict, 21 top/PachetoK/, 21 bottom/MrIncredible, 24–25/ivan_kislitsin, 26 top/Bellawillow Photography, 26 center/JIB Liverpool, 26 bottom/Nesolenaya Alexandra, 27/Myimagine, 32/HelloRF Zcool, 35/Timcharinee, 50/Anna Malygina, 51/Konstantins Pobilojs, 55/aniana, 62/offish25,64/Piti Tan, 34, 66/tarapong srichaiyos, 130/pui_bunny, 39, 76, 188, 220/Sanit Fuangnakhon, 68–69, 230–31/Africa Studio, 232/Protasov AN, 233/NOPPHARAT STUDIO62, 234/PopFoto, 235 top/Kinoya